JESUS CHRIST

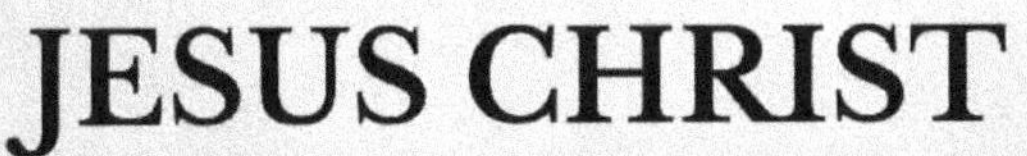

The Great Teacher

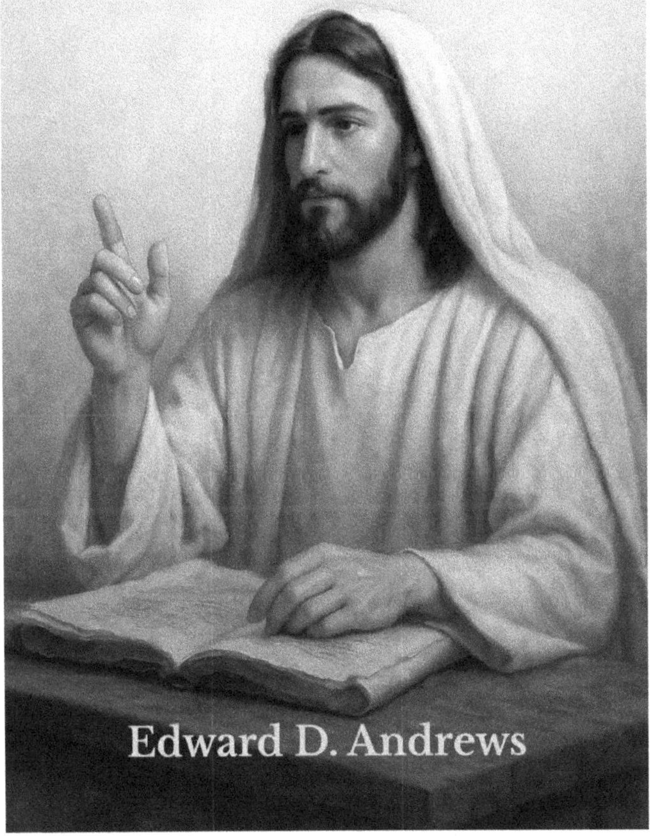

Edward D. Andrews

JESUS CHRIST

The Great Teacher

"Go therefore and make disciples ... teaching them to observe all that I commanded you ..." – Matthew 28:19-20

Edward D. Andrews

Christian Publishing House

Cambridge, Ohio

support@christianpublishers.org

JESUS CHRIST: The Great Teacher by Edward D. Andrews

ISBN-10: 1949586839

ISBN-13: 978-1949586831

Table of Contents

PREFACE

Every generation of Christians faces the same command and the same challenge—*"Go therefore and make disciples ... teaching them to observe all that I have commanded you"* (Matthew 28:19–20). The heart of this commission is teaching. The strength of the Church has always rested upon the faithful transmission of biblical truth from one believer to another. In every era, when teaching has weakened, faith has waned; when teaching has flourished, the gospel has advanced.

This book, ***Jesus Christ: The Great Teacher***, was written to rekindle that essential calling. It seeks to help believers not only understand the teaching methods of Jesus but to imitate them—to teach as He taught, with clarity, authority, compassion, and conviction. Jesus was not simply a preacher of truth; He was its perfect embodiment. His words illuminated Scripture, His logic refuted error, His questions provoked repentance, and His parables transformed ordinary moments into eternal lessons.

In an age marked by moral confusion, shallow doctrine, and a growing indifference to truth, Christians must once again take up the Teacher's mantle. The modern world is overflowing with information yet starving for wisdom. The only cure is a return to the inspired Word of God, faithfully explained and courageously applied. Teachers of the Word today must combine sound exegesis with the love and patience of Christ Himself.

This work is not a theoretical study. It is a manual for discipleship and a guide for those who desire to communicate God's Word effectively. Each chapter examines an aspect of Jesus' teaching—His simplicity, His use of questions and illustrations, His mastery of logic, His compassion, and His unwavering devotion to the Father's will. Together, these chapters form a portrait of divine pedagogy—the perfect model for every Christian who would teach others.

Whether you are a pastor, missionary, Bible study leader, parent, or new believer desiring to grow, this book will help you follow the footsteps of the Great Teacher. Its purpose is not to elevate human technique, but to glorify the One who is the Truth itself. May every reader finish this book more determined to learn from Christ, live like Christ, and teach for Christ—until His truth fills the earth.

Edward D. Andrews

Author of 220 books and Chief Translator of the Updated American Standard Version

Introduction: The Urgent Need for Biblical Teachers

The Church of Jesus Christ stands at a pivotal point in history. The twenty-first century has seen both unprecedented opportunity and unparalleled confusion concerning truth, authority, and Scripture. False teachings multiply rapidly, secular ideologies increasingly shape the moral compass of society, and many within the Church struggle to articulate what they believe and why. This environment demands an urgent response from faithful believers—men and women who will rise as skilled teachers of God's Word, equipped to instruct others with the clarity, compassion, and conviction of Jesus Christ Himself, the Great Teacher.

In this age of doctrinal compromise, the calling to teach biblically has never been more vital. Christianity is not sustained by emotional experience, cultural relevance, or institutional tradition, but by the accurate teaching of the inspired Word of God. It was teaching—not miracles—that most characterized Jesus' ministry. He preached to multitudes, but He discipled through teaching. His every word and action reflected divine wisdom, truth, and purpose.

Christians today must follow that same pattern: to evangelize, disciple, and defend the faith by teaching exactly what God has revealed in Scripture.

The Mission to Teach and Evangelize

From the beginning of His ministry, Jesus identified His mission as that of a Teacher. The Gospels record Him continually addressing crowds, instructing disciples, explaining the Scriptures, and proclaiming the Kingdom of God. "Jesus went about all Galilee, teaching in their synagogues, and proclaiming the gospel of the kingdom" (Matthew 4:23). Teaching was not an occasional aspect of His ministry—it was its essence. He revealed divine truths to the humble, exposed hypocrisy among the religious elite, and formed disciples who would carry His message to the ends of the earth.

That same mission continues through the Church today. Teaching and evangelism are inseparable. True evangelism is not merely telling others about Christ—it is training them in His teachings. Jesus commanded, "Go therefore and make disciples of all nations... teaching them to observe all that I have commanded you" (Matthew 28:19–20). To "make disciples" means to cultivate learners who follow Jesus' words, live by His teachings, and reflect

His character. Evangelism introduces the sinner to salvation; teaching establishes the believer in truth. Together, they form the twofold duty of every faithful Christian—proclaim and instruct.

The Apostle Paul viewed this mission as the heartbeat of his ministry: "For I did not shrink from declaring to you the whole purpose of God" (Acts 20:27). His goal was not simply to convert but to teach "Christ in all wisdom, so that we may present every man complete in Christ" (Colossians 1:28). The modern Church must recover this biblical emphasis. We do not merely need more preachers—we need teachers who will unfold the Scriptures accurately, systematically, and fearlessly, imitating the teaching model of Jesus Christ.

The Call to Defend the Faith Through Scripture

Teaching and defending the faith are inseparable duties of every Christian leader. To teach truth necessarily means to expose error. The Apostle Peter urged believers to "sanctify Christ as Lord in your hearts, always being ready to make a defense to everyone who asks you to give an account for the hope that is in you" (1 Peter 3:15). This defense, or *apologia*, requires both knowledge and humility—

knowledge of God's Word and humility of spirit in its presentation.

The Church is surrounded by intellectual and moral opposition. Secular philosophies, liberal theology, and false religions challenge the inspiration, inerrancy, and authority of Scripture. Many churchgoers lack the biblical grounding to withstand such attacks. They have zeal but little knowledge; sincerity but not accuracy. As a result, false teachers flourish and unbiblical movements thrive.

Biblical teaching is the Church's greatest defense against deception. When God's Word is rightly handled, it exposes the counterfeit. The Apostle Paul told Titus that church leaders must "hold firmly to the faithful word... so that they will be able both to exhort in sound doctrine and to refute those who contradict" (Titus 1:9). Defending the faith begins with teaching the Word correctly. Every believer who teaches—even in small settings like home Bible studies or personal evangelism—stands as a guardian of divine truth.

To defend Scripture effectively, we must know it deeply. Defense without knowledge leads to confusion; knowledge without devotion leads to arrogance. The biblical teacher must unite both—accurate understanding and spiritual maturity.

Through diligent study, prayer, and obedience, he or she becomes a vessel through whom Jehovah's truth flows to others.

Evangelism and Apologetics Defined

Evangelism and apologetics are two sides of the same divine calling. Evangelism proclaims the truth of the gospel; apologetics explains and defends it. Both were integral to Jesus' ministry and to the apostolic mission that followed. The Greek word *euangelion* means "good news." To evangelize is to announce God's good news of salvation through Jesus Christ—His death, resurrection, and promised return. This message confronts sin, calls for repentance, and offers eternal life through faith in Christ.

Apologetics, from the Greek *apologia*, means "a reasoned defense." It does not seek to argue for argument's sake but to clarify truth and remove obstacles that hinder belief. When Paul reasoned in the synagogues, he was both evangelizing and defending: "He reasoned with them from the Scriptures, explaining and giving evidence that the Christ had to suffer and rise again" (Acts 17:2–3).

Thus, apologetics supports evangelism by preparing the ground for faith. It answers objections, corrects misconceptions, and builds confidence in the trustworthiness of the Bible. When unbelievers encounter confusion or hostility toward Scripture, apologetics gently but firmly brings them back to the Word of God. Evangelism without apologetics lacks depth; apologetics without evangelism lacks love. The biblical teacher unites both—reasoning persuasively from Scripture and inviting sinners to repentance.

Pre-Evangelism: Preparing Hearts and Minds

Before a person can receive the message of salvation, their heart and mind must be prepared. This preparatory work is known as pre-evangelism. It involves removing intellectual and emotional barriers that prevent people from hearing the truth. Jesus often engaged in pre-evangelism before presenting the full gospel. He corrected false ideas, exposed hypocrisy, and provoked thought through questions and parables.

Consider His encounter with the Samaritan woman in John 4. Jesus began by engaging her curiosity ("Give Me a drink"), then led her to recognize her need for living water, and finally revealed Himself as the Messiah. This gradual unveiling of truth illustrates pre-evangelism. The hearer must first see their spiritual thirst before they can appreciate the water of life.

Modern teachers and evangelists must adopt this same patience and discernment. Before confronting unbelief, they must understand it. Before teaching truth, they must prepare the ground. Pre-evangelism is not compromise—it is compassion. It recognizes that most people today are far removed from biblical literacy. We must first awaken their conscience, clarify misconceptions, and lead them to consider the claims of Christ seriously. When the heart is ready, the seed of the Word can take root and bear fruit.

The Biblical Model of Teaching and Discipleship

Jesus' model for teaching was deeply relational and intentional. He taught the crowds publicly but discipled a few privately. He spoke truth clearly but lived it consistently. He invited His followers not merely to learn His words but to imitate His life. "Take My yoke upon you and learn from Me" (Matthew 11:29). To learn from Jesus meant to walk with Him daily—to hear, observe, and obey.

The early Church followed this pattern. The apostles did not rely on mere intellectual instruction but on continuous life-sharing discipleship. They equipped others who would, in turn, teach others: "The things which you have heard from me... entrust these to faithful men who will be able to teach others also" (2 Timothy 2:2). True discipleship multiplies teachers. Every Christian who grows in knowledge and faith should pass that knowledge to others.

Biblical teaching and discipleship go hand in hand. Teaching informs the mind; discipleship transforms the life. Together, they form the process by which believers mature and reproduce spiritually. The Church does not grow through entertainment or emotional appeal but through systematic, Scripture-centered teaching that produces obedient followers of Christ.

All Christians Share in the Evangelism Mandate

The Great Commission was not given to pastors alone—it was given to all disciples. Every Christian, regardless of gifting or position, is called to participate in evangelism and teaching. "Let the word of Christ dwell in you richly, teaching and admonishing one another in all wisdom" (Colossians 3:16). Some are full-time teachers and evangelists, but all are witnesses. Every believer's life and words must point others to the truth of God's Word.

The early Church understood this collective responsibility. Ordinary Christians—merchants, mothers, servants, and soldiers—carried the gospel wherever they went. By the year 125 C.E., historians estimate that there were over one million Christians in the Roman Empire. This rapid growth was not the result of professional clergy but of everyday believers obeying Christ's command to teach and make disciples.

Today's Church must recapture that same zeal. Evangelism is not an optional ministry for a few; it is the natural expression of genuine faith. Every believer who studies, applies, and teaches Scripture becomes a link in the divine chain of truth stretching from Christ to the present. The world desperately needs teachers who will handle God's Word accurately and share it courageously.

The need is urgent. False teachers multiply. Souls perish in ignorance. Many churches have replaced expository teaching with motivational speaking. But God still calls faithful servants who will say, "Here am I; send me." Biblical teachers must rise—men and women filled not with their own ideas but with the living Word of God, ready to teach, defend, and disciple as Jesus Christ did.

Chapter 1: Becoming Adequately Qualified to Teach Others

The command to teach the Word of God is not a suggestion; it is a sacred obligation laid upon every believer who bears the name of Christ. In 2 Timothy 2:2, the Apostle Paul charged Timothy, "And the things which you have heard from me in the presence of many witnesses, entrust these to faithful men who will be adequately qualified to teach others also." This statement lays the foundation for every faithful teacher of the Scriptures. The Christian's calling is not simply to believe, but to learn, live, and then teach the truth to others. In this way, the truth of Jehovah's Word is multiplied through generation after generation of disciples.

However, to be a teacher of God's Word requires more than enthusiasm or good intentions. It demands preparation, faithfulness, and skill. One must become *adequately qualified*—not merely through human education but through a deep understanding and application of Scripture. Paul's instruction implies a process of training, discipline, and devotion, by which a believer grows from learner to teacher.

Jesus Christ, the Great Teacher, exemplified this standard. He was not self-appointed but divinely commissioned and perfectly equipped to communicate the truth of God. Though we can never teach with His perfection, we are called to imitate His devotion, His method, and His love for truth.

The Meaning of "Adequately Qualified" (2 Timothy 2:2)

To understand what it means to be "adequately qualified," we must consider the Greek term *hikanos*, which conveys the idea of being competent, sufficient, or fit for a specific purpose. Paul's use of this word implies that teaching is not for the unprepared or casual believer. The teacher must be spiritually mature, doctrinally sound, and practically equipped to communicate divine truth accurately.

Teaching God's Word is not merely sharing one's opinions about the Bible; it is conveying the very thoughts of Jehovah as revealed through Scripture. Therefore, qualification to teach does not come from human charisma, public speaking skill, or emotional appeal—it comes from being firmly grounded in truth and living in obedience to it.

Paul instructed Timothy to find "faithful men" who could be trained to teach others. Faithfulness and ability are the two pillars of biblical qualification. Faithfulness means reliability, consistency, and devotion to God's truth. Ability refers to the skill acquired through study, reflection, and practice. To be adequately qualified is to combine both—the heart of devotion and the mind of discernment.

The teacher who is adequately qualified understands the Scriptures in their context, discerns their meaning through the guidance of the Holy Spirit in the Word, and communicates them clearly and accurately. He is not merely a transmitter of information but a steward of truth, entrusted with the sacred responsibility to guard and proclaim the Word of God without distortion.

Faithfulness and Knowledge in the Teacher

In Paul's second letter to Timothy, the apostle emphasized not only competence but character. The spiritual qualifications of a teacher begin with faithfulness. "It is required of stewards that they be found faithful" (1 Corinthians 4:2). The faithful teacher lives what he teaches. His credibility comes from consistency. He cannot instruct others to obey Christ while living contrary to the truth himself.

Faithfulness is also expressed in perseverance. Teaching God's Word requires endurance through opposition, discouragement, and spiritual resistance. Paul warned Timothy that "the time will come when they will not endure sound teaching" (2 Timothy 4:3). Yet the faithful teacher continues, not for applause or recognition, but out of loyalty to Jehovah and His truth.

Alongside faithfulness, the teacher must possess knowledge—accurate, deep, and growing knowledge of Scripture. Proverbs 19:2 warns, "It is not good for a person to be without knowledge." Zeal without understanding leads to error. The teacher must "do [his] best to present [himself] to God as one approved, a workman who does not need to be ashamed, rightly handling the word of truth" (2 Timothy 2:15).

This knowledge is not merely academic; it is experiential and spiritual. It is acquired through diligent study, prayerful meditation, and personal obedience. As the teacher grows in the Word, his ability to feed others increases. He becomes not only a student of the Scriptures but a living demonstration of their power.

Skillfully Handling the Word of Truth

To "rightly handle the word of truth" means to interpret and apply Scripture correctly. The Greek term *orthotomeō* literally means "to cut straight." The idea is that of precision and accuracy—handling the Word in a way that preserves its intended meaning.

A teacher who misuses Scripture can do great harm, even unintentionally. Twisting verses out of context or imposing human traditions upon divine revelation distorts truth and leads listeners astray. Peter warned that "the untaught and unstable distort [the Scriptures], as they do also the rest of the Scriptures, to their own destruction" (2 Peter 3:16).

The faithful teacher therefore studies carefully. He considers the grammatical, historical, and literary context of every passage. He compares Scripture with Scripture, allowing the Bible to interpret itself. He understands that the Word of God is a unified revelation, not a collection of disconnected sayings. He does not seek new or novel interpretations but strives to uncover the original meaning as intended by the inspired writers.

Right handling of the Word also includes proper application. Knowledge must lead to obedience. A teacher who rightly divides the Word not only interprets it correctly but also lives it consistently. His teaching has integrity because his life aligns with his message.

The Christian's Spiritual Training and Growth

Becoming adequately qualified to teach involves lifelong spiritual training. Just as a soldier must be disciplined to handle his weapon effectively, the Christian must be trained to use "the sword of the Spirit, which is the word of God" (Ephesians 6:17).

Spiritual training begins with personal devotion to study and prayer. The believer who neglects the Word cannot hope to teach it. Paul urged Timothy to "continue in the things you have learned and become convinced of" (2 Timothy 3:14). Growth in understanding comes through consistent exposure to Scripture, reflection upon its meaning, and application in daily life.

Training also involves humility and correction. Even the most mature teacher must remain teachable. Apollos, though "mighty in the Scriptures," was willing to receive further instruction from Aquila and Priscilla (Acts 18:24–26). The teacher who refuses correction endangers both himself and his hearers.

Furthermore, spiritual growth comes through trials and perseverance. Teaching often exposes the believer to spiritual opposition, discouragement, and criticism. Yet these experiences refine the teacher's character and deepen his reliance upon God. Every challenge becomes an opportunity to learn patience, wisdom, and compassion.

The Role of Teaching in Spiritual Warfare

Paul reminded Timothy that believers are engaged in a continual spiritual battle. Teaching the truth of God's Word is one of the most powerful weapons in this warfare. "For the weapons of our warfare are not of the flesh, but divinely powerful for the destruction of fortresses" (2 Corinthians 10:4). False doctrines, worldly philosophies, and moral corruption are spiritual strongholds that can only be torn down by the truth of Scripture.

The Christian teacher stands on the front line of this battle. His task is not merely to inform but to defend—to expose falsehood and proclaim truth. Satan's primary tactic is deception, and the teacher's defense is accurate doctrine. When the Word of God is taught clearly and authoritatively, error is exposed, and believers are strengthened to resist temptation.

This warfare demands courage and vigilance. Teachers must be "sober-minded, enduring hardship, doing the work of an evangelist" (2 Timothy 4:5).

Teaching is not a comfortable task; it invites opposition from both the world and the forces of darkness. Yet the faithful teacher takes his stand with the armor of God, confident that truth will prevail.

Combining Knowledge, Belief, and Obedience

The effective teacher unites three essential elements: knowledge, belief, and obedience. Knowledge without belief becomes sterile intellectualism. Belief without knowledge degenerates into emotionalism. Obedience without understanding produces legalism. But when all three are joined, they form the foundation of authentic Christian teaching.

Knowledge gives the teacher accuracy, belief gives conviction, and obedience gives credibility. The teacher must know the truth, believe it wholeheartedly, and live it faithfully. Only then can his teaching carry spiritual authority and power.

Paul's charge to Timothy captures this balance: "Pay close attention to yourself and to your teaching; persevere in these things, for as you do this you will ensure salvation both for yourself and for those who hear you" (1 Timothy 4:16). Teaching begins with the teacher's own life. Before we can teach others, we must first teach ourselves—submitting our thoughts, actions, and motives to the Word of God.

When knowledge, belief, and obedience align, the teacher becomes a living example of truth. His words carry weight not because of eloquence but because of authenticity. He teaches not only from Scripture but from a transformed heart.

The Church today urgently needs teachers who embody these qualities—faithful, skilled, and spiritually mature servants who rightly handle the Word of truth. The call to teach is a sacred trust. Those who accept it must devote themselves to study, prayer, holiness, and perseverance. To be "adequately qualified" is to be wholly surrendered to the authority of God's Word, ready to teach others as Christ, the Great Teacher, has taught us.

Chapter 2: Why Jesus Was the Greatest Teacher

No teacher in history has equaled Jesus Christ in wisdom, authority, and transformative power. His words transcended human understanding, pierced the conscience, and redefined righteousness. Jesus did not simply convey information—He imparted divine truth with eternal significance. His influence has shaped every generation, every culture, and every sincere student of Scripture. The Gospels record that "the crowds were amazed at His teaching; for He was teaching them as one having authority, and not as their scribes" (Matthew 7:28–29). This distinction is the key to understanding why Jesus was, and remains, the greatest Teacher who ever lived.

Unlike the teachers of His day, Jesus spoke not as a mere interpreter of the Law, but as its Author and fulfillment. His every word carried divine weight, because He taught as the incarnate Word of God (John 1:14). His authority flowed not from education or human ordination, but from His identity as the Son of God. Yet His teaching also revealed profound humility, compassion, and accessibility. He taught heavenly truths in earthly language, engaging the hearts of farmers and fishermen as well as scholars and rulers.

This chapter explores six defining qualities that made Jesus the supreme model for every Christian teacher—His divine origin, His authority, His love for truth and humanity, His scriptural literacy, His humility, and His lifelong mission to teach and make disciples.

Jesus' Divine Origin and Infinite Knowledge

The source of Jesus' teaching was His divine origin. He was not a man discovering truth but God revealing it. "My teaching is not Mine, but His who sent Me" (John 7:16). As the eternal Word, Jesus possessed infinite knowledge of all things—the human heart, the will of the Father, and the realities of both heaven and earth. His teaching was not speculative; it was absolute revelation.

When Jesus taught, He did not cite external authorities to validate His words, as the rabbis did. They quoted long chains of tradition—"Rabbi so-and-so said..."—but Jesus spoke directly, "Truly, truly, I say to you." This phrase, unique to His speech, affirmed His divine insight. He taught as One who knew, not as one who guessed.

Jesus' divine knowledge also extended to the hearts of His listeners. "He Himself knew what was in man" (John 2:25). His teaching reached beyond the intellect to expose motives, desires, and sins. When He spoke, truth confronted the soul. The woman at the well, the rich young ruler, and Nicodemus each discovered that His words penetrated the deepest recesses of their being.

Unlike human teachers who learn through experience, Jesus' understanding was immediate and complete. Yet He conveyed divine truths in ways that finite minds could grasp. He adapted infinite knowledge to human limitation, translating heavenly wisdom into earthly expression. His divine omniscience, clothed in perfect love, made Him the ultimate communicator of truth.

Teaching With Authority, Not Tradition

In the first century, Jewish religious instruction was bound by the traditions of the elders. Teachers relied upon precedent rather than Scripture's inherent power. Jesus broke through this lifeless pattern. His authority derived directly from Jehovah, not from human endorsement.

When the people heard Him, they immediately recognized this difference. Matthew writes, “He was teaching them as one having authority, and not as their scribes” (Matthew 7:29). The Greek word for “authority” (*exousia*) means rightful power or inherent ability to command. Jesus’ authority was intrinsic—it came from who He was. He did not need to appeal to external sources; His words carried divine force.

This authority astonished His audiences. They said, “Never has a man spoken the way this man speaks” (John 7:46). His teaching silenced critics, comforted the brokenhearted, and awakened consciences. He could say, “You have heard that it was said... but I say to you” (Matthew 5:21–22), establishing divine interpretation above human commentary.

Authority without arrogance was one of Jesus’ defining marks. He was confident, never defensive; decisive, never domineering. His authority attracted the humble and exposed the proud. It inspired trust because it reflected perfect alignment with the Father’s will. “I do nothing on My own initiative, but I speak these things as the Father taught Me” (John 8:28).

Every true Christian teacher must mirror this principle. Authority in teaching comes not from titles or institutions but from faithful submission to God's Word. When a teacher speaks the Scriptures accurately, the Word itself carries divine authority. The task of the teacher, therefore, is to echo Christ's voice—nothing more, nothing less.

His Love for Truth and Humanity

Jesus' teaching flowed from perfect love—love for the truth of God and love for the souls of men. These two loves were never in conflict but harmonized in every word He spoke. "Grace and truth came through Jesus Christ" (John 1:17). His instruction was never detached, never merely academic. He taught because He loved, and He loved by teaching.

His love for truth was absolute. He never compromised doctrine to please listeners or avoid conflict. Even when His words offended, He refused to dilute them. When many disciples turned away after His hard sayings, Jesus asked the Twelve, "Do you also want to go away?" (John 6:67). His teaching was governed by truth, not popularity.

At the same time, His love for people shaped the tone of His teaching. He was "gentle and humble in heart" (Matthew 11:29). He understood human weakness and tailored His words accordingly. To the sinner, He offered mercy; to the hypocrite, correction; to the seeking heart, guidance. His love did not manifest as indulgence but as patient, restorative truth.

Consider His interaction with the woman caught in adultery. He neither condoned her sin nor condemned her person. "Neither do I condemn you; go and sin no more" (John 8:11). That balance—grace coupled with moral clarity—is the mark of perfect teaching.

Every faithful teacher must learn this pattern. Love for truth prevents compromise; love for people prevents cruelty. The teacher who loves both will instruct with conviction and compassion, following the example of the Master.

His Literacy, Learning, and Use of Scripture

Although Jesus was not trained in rabbinic schools, He was fully literate and profoundly learned in Scripture. When He read from the scroll of Isaiah in the synagogue (Luke 4:16–21), He demonstrated precise knowledge of the text and its prophetic fulfillment. His education came not from men but from divine communion with the Father and the careful study of Scripture from His youth.

Jesus' use of Scripture was both authoritative and insightful. He quoted from all three major divisions of the Hebrew Bible—Law, Prophets, and Writings—and used them in perfect harmony. In His temptations, He defeated Satan solely by citing Scripture: "It is written" (Matthew 4:4, 7, 10). This reveals not only His memorization but His deep comprehension of context and intent.

When teaching, He frequently began with Scripture, unfolded its meaning, and applied it to life. On the road to Emmaus, "He explained to them the things concerning Himself in all the Scriptures" (Luke 24:27). His interpretation was neither allegorical nor speculative but literal and precise, unveiling the continuity of God's redemptive plan.

Jesus' literacy also demonstrated respect for the written Word. He treated Scripture as the final authority, never questioning its inspiration or reliability. "The Scripture cannot be broken" (John 10:35). For Him, to teach apart from Scripture was unthinkable.

This literacy and reverence for the Word set the standard for all teachers who would follow Him. True teaching requires both understanding and submission. The teacher who does not know Scripture cannot rightly represent its Author. Jesus' example shows that the most powerful teaching begins with mastery of the text and ends with obedience to it.

Humility and Focus on the Father's Will

Despite His divine nature and absolute authority, Jesus modeled perfect humility. He never sought personal recognition or human praise. "My food is to do the will of Him who sent Me and to accomplish His work" (John 4:34). Every word He spoke, every miracle He performed, and every lesson He taught flowed from this unwavering submission to the Father's will.

Humility was the foundation of His authority. Though He could have demanded worship from all creation, He chose the form of a servant. "He humbled Himself by becoming obedient to the point of death, even death on a cross" (Philippians 2:8). His humility was not weakness—it was strength under control, guided by perfect obedience.

As a teacher, this humility made Him approachable. The poor, the broken, and the outcast felt safe in His presence. He never elevated Himself above His students but invited them to learn alongside Him: "Take My yoke upon you and learn from Me" (Matthew 11:29). The imagery of a shared yoke suggests partnership, not hierarchy.

In this, Jesus provided the ultimate model for all teachers. Pride corrupts teaching; humility purifies it. The teacher's goal is not to impress but to instruct—not to glorify self, but to glorify God. When humility governs the heart, the focus remains where it belongs—on the truth of God's Word and the will of the Father.

Christ's Mission: To Teach and Make Disciples

Teaching was not incidental to Jesus' mission; it was central. From the beginning of His ministry to its end, He prioritized instruction. "Jesus went about all Galilee, teaching in their synagogues, proclaiming the gospel of the kingdom, and healing every disease" (Matthew 4:23). Healing and miracles confirmed His message, but teaching conveyed its substance.

Jesus' mission as Teacher culminated in His final command: "Go therefore and make disciples of all nations... teaching them to observe all that I commanded you" (Matthew 28:19–20). His earthly ministry began with teaching the multitudes and ended with commissioning others to continue that teaching. The continuity underscores its eternal importance.

Discipleship, in Jesus' model, is inseparable from teaching. A disciple is a learner who becomes a doer. Jesus' goal was not to create followers dependent on Him physically but to produce mature believers dependent on God's Word. He taught them principles, demonstrated them, and then sent them to replicate His example.

This mission continues through the Church. Every believer is called to participate in this teaching chain—learning from the Word, living its truth, and transmitting it to others. The teacher's role is vital, not because of personal prestige, but because it carries forward the mission of Christ Himself.

In every sense, Jesus was and remains the greatest Teacher. His divine knowledge, authority, compassion, humility, and obedience combine into the perfect model of instruction. To teach as He taught is the highest calling and the greatest privilege bestowed upon the servants of God.

Chapter 3: The Teaching Power of the Gospel of Matthew

The Gospel of Matthew reveals Jesus Christ as both Messiah and Master Teacher. More than any other Gospel writer, Matthew highlights the teaching ministry of Jesus—His authority in instruction, His clarity in communication, and His divine wisdom that transcended human learning. The Gospel's structure itself testifies to this emphasis, containing five major discourses (chapters 5–7; 10; 13; 18; 24–25), each ending with the phrase, "When Jesus had finished these sayings." These discourses mirror the five books of Moses, demonstrating that Jesus is the greater Lawgiver and Teacher who brings divine truth to its fulfillment.

Within Matthew, the Sermon on the Mount (chapters 5–7) stands as the pinnacle of Jesus' teaching. It distills the essence of righteous living under the rule of God and reveals the simplicity, depth, and spiritual power that characterized Jesus' method of instruction. The Sermon is not a theoretical lecture but a living guide to discipleship—

a framework for evangelism, spiritual growth, and moral transformation.

Through the Gospel of Matthew, we witness how Jesus' teaching methods combined divine authority with human accessibility. His words were never hollow philosophy; they carried eternal weight and personal relevance. He addressed the mind, stirred the conscience, and moved the heart. The effectiveness of His teaching in Matthew lies in its simplicity, its clarity, and its transforming power.

The Sermon on the Mount and Its Simplicity

The Sermon on the Mount begins with a breathtaking simplicity that masks profound theological truth. "Blessed are the poor in spirit, for theirs is the kingdom of the heavens" (Matthew 5:3). With this opening beatitude, Jesus reverses human expectations and lays the foundation for His entire message. In a few sentences, He dismantles the self-righteousness of the Pharisees and reveals the inner disposition that God approves—a humble, contrite spirit that depends wholly upon Him.

Jesus' sermon was not a complex philosophical discourse. It was a direct, Spirit-inspired message that spoke to the hearts of ordinary people—farmers, fishermen, and families who had little formal education but great spiritual hunger. His words were straightforward, yet profound. They were short, yet unforgettable. His audience could not only understand Him; they could remember and repeat His teachings.

The simplicity of Jesus' teaching was never a result of shallowness, but of perfect clarity. He understood human nature—the need for vivid imagery, repetition, and moral relevance. While religious leaders buried truth beneath traditions and legal minutiae, Jesus unveiled the heart of God's law in language so simple a child could grasp it. "You have heard that it was said... But I say to you" (Matthew 5:21–22). In those words, Jesus revealed divine authority clothed in simplicity.

The Sermon's structure itself demonstrates perfect instructional design. It begins with character (the Beatitudes), proceeds to influence (salt and light), moves into practical righteousness (obedience to God's law from the heart), and concludes with the call to decision (building on the rock). This logical flow is a model for every teacher of the Word—start with transformation of heart, then expand to transformation of conduct.

Use of Short, Memorable Beatitudes

The Beatitudes (Matthew 5:3–12) represent one of the most masterful uses of brevity in Scripture. Each statement begins with the word "Blessed" (*makarios*), meaning deep spiritual joy, fulfillment, or divine favor. Jesus compresses entire theological truths into concise, rhythmic sentences that the listener could easily recall.

These blessings describe not worldly happiness but the inward condition of those who belong to the kingdom of God. In each, Jesus connects attitude with reward—poverty of spirit with heavenly inheritance, mourning with comfort, meekness with dominion, mercy with mercy, and purity with the vision of God. The Beatitudes are not random virtues but progressive steps of spiritual maturity.

In teaching, Jesus models an essential principle: **truth that endures must be truth that can be remembered.** Short, memorable statements enable listeners to retain spiritual truth long after the teacher is gone. The Beatitudes became the cornerstone of Christian ethics, shaping not only personal holiness but also the Church's moral foundation throughout history.

Furthermore, Jesus' repetition of "Blessed are..." engraves divine approval into the hearts of His disciples. It reminds every believer that God's blessing is not found in worldly status or success, but in humility, righteousness, mercy, and faithfulness. By constructing these truths as compact, poetic lines, Jesus equipped His hearers to internalize and share them. The Beatitudes are portable theology—truth small enough to carry in the memory, yet deep enough to fill eternity.

Commandments Communicated Clearly

One of Jesus' greatest accomplishments as a teacher was His ability to simplify divine law without diminishing its authority. He made the eternal principles of righteousness understandable and practical for daily life. In Matthew 5:21–48, Jesus provides six examples contrasting the external legalism of the scribes with the internal righteousness God requires: anger versus murder, lust versus adultery, oaths versus truthfulness, retaliation versus forgiveness, and hatred versus love.

Each contrast follows a pattern of direct comparison: "You have heard that it was said... but I say to you." With this formula, Jesus asserts His divine authority over human tradition. He does not abolish the law but fulfills it by restoring its true intent—love from a pure heart.

For instance, when addressing the commandment against murder, Jesus deepens it to include anger and insult: "Everyone who is angry with his brother shall be guilty before the court" (Matthew 5:22). He shows that righteousness is not merely outward obedience but inner transformation. Similarly, when addressing adultery, He declares, "Everyone who looks at a woman with lust for her has already committed adultery with her in his heart" (Matthew 5:28).

Through these teachings, Jesus accomplishes what few teachers achieve: He elevates the moral standard while increasing accessibility. He uses simple language to convey profound spiritual realities. He teaches that holiness is not confined to ritual but is rooted in motive. His clear commandments pierce through centuries of distortion and reveal the heart of God's law—a righteousness that exceeds that of the scribes and Pharisees (Matthew 5:20).

For the Christian teacher today, Jesus' example reminds us that clarity honors truth. The clearer our communication, the stronger our impact. Truth loses power when clouded by jargon, speculation, or ambiguity. Like Jesus, we must speak plainly and truthfully, ensuring that our words illuminate rather than obscure the Word of God.

Visual and Verbal Illustrations

Jesus' teaching in Matthew is rich with vivid imagery and concrete illustrations. He understood the power of mental pictures in conveying eternal truths. His audience lived close to the land—they understood farming, building, fishing, and family life. By drawing from their experience, Jesus transformed ordinary scenes into spiritual lessons.

He spoke of salt and light (Matthew 5:13–16), lamps and bushels, trees and fruit (7:17–20), birds and lilies (6:26–28), and houses built on rock or sand (7:24–27). Each illustration provided a visual anchor for spiritual concepts, turning abstract truths into visible realities.

For example, when Jesus said, "You are the light of the world," His listeners could easily picture the lamps flickering in their homes or the city on a hill visible in the distance. The image conveyed identity and purpose—they were to shine with the truth of God in a darkened world.

Visual and verbal illustrations work together to engage both the intellect and imagination. They awaken understanding, aid memory, and invite reflection. Jesus did not lecture His audience with sterile propositions; He painted living portraits of truth. The result was that His words penetrated the heart, not just the mind.

For modern teachers and evangelists, the lesson is clear: use imagery drawn from everyday life to reveal divine principles. The farmer's field, the craftsman's hands, the parent's love—all become teaching tools when connected to Scripture. A single picture often conveys more truth than a hundred sentences.

Persuasive Questions and Rebukes

Jesus frequently employed questions—not to gain information but to provoke reflection and expose false thinking. His teaching in Matthew is filled with carefully crafted questions that force listeners to confront their motives and beliefs. "For what will it profit a man if he gains the whole world and forfeits his soul?" (Matthew 16:26). No statement could more powerfully expose misplaced priorities.

He also used questions to disarm critics and reveal hypocrisy. When the Pharisees asked whether it was lawful to heal on the Sabbath, Jesus responded, "What man will there be among you who will have one sheep, and if it falls into a pit on the Sabbath, will he not take hold of it and lift it out?" (Matthew 12:11). His question left them speechless and demonstrated that mercy fulfills the law.

Even His rebukes were instructional. When Peter, driven by emotion, tried to prevent Jesus' death, the Lord said, "Get behind Me, Satan! You are a stumbling block to Me" (Matthew 16:23). Though stern, the rebuke was corrective—it taught Peter that God's purposes transcend human reasoning.

The combination of probing questions and firm rebukes reveals the balance in Jesus' teaching: compassion without compromise, gentleness without weakness, and authority without arrogance. His questions turned passive listeners into active thinkers. His rebukes, though severe, always led toward restoration and truth.

Teachers today must learn to use questions that engage the conscience and rebukes that correct without crushing. A well-placed question can open a closed heart; a gentle correction can save a soul from error. In the hands of a godly teacher, both are tools of divine persuasion.

Training Listeners to Teach Others

One of the greatest indicators of effective teaching is reproduction—the ability to raise others who can, in turn, teach the truth. Jesus' ministry in Matthew demonstrates this principle clearly. His goal was not merely to inform but to transform disciples into teachers who would continue His mission after His departure.

In Matthew 28:19–20, the Great Commission encapsulates the entire teaching purpose of Christ: "Go therefore and make disciples of all nations... teaching them to observe all that I commanded you." Notice the progression: making disciples includes baptizing and teaching. The task of the Church is not complete when someone believes; it continues as we train them to live and teach the Word.

Throughout Matthew, Jesus prepared His disciples for this mission. He modeled teaching (chapters 5–7), sent them on supervised missions (chapter 10), explained parables privately (chapter 13), and instructed them about humility, forgiveness, and discipline (chapter 18). By the end of His ministry, they were ready to teach others as He had taught them.

This model of multiplication is essential for the Church today. Every Christian who learns must also teach. Every pastor must train others to handle the Word faithfully. The truth must not end with us but flow through us to others. Paul applied this principle directly: "The things which you have heard from me... entrust these to faithful men who will be able to teach others also" (2 Timothy 2:2).

Thus, Jesus' teaching in Matthew does more than convey doctrine—it establishes a legacy of learning and teaching that continues through every generation of faithful believers.

The Gospel of Matthew reveals that the power of Jesus' teaching lay not merely in what He said, but in how He said it—with simplicity, clarity, vivid imagery, logical reasoning, and moral authority. His words continue to train, transform, and commission His followers. Every teacher of the Word must study this Gospel carefully, for within its pages lies the supreme model of instruction—*Jesus Christ, the Great Teacher*.

Chapter 4: Teaching With Simplicity and Clarity

One of the most remarkable aspects of Jesus' teaching was His ability to communicate eternal truths in simple, clear, and memorable language. His teachings reached the unlearned and the intellectual alike, cutting through centuries of tradition and speculation. He spoke not to impress, but to illuminate; not to obscure, but to reveal. In an age when religious leaders multiplied words and complicated God's truth with human traditions, Jesus restored divine teaching to its pure and understandable form.

The simplicity and clarity of His instruction were not signs of shallowness but of supreme mastery. Only one who fully understands a subject can present it simply. The greatest Teacher who ever lived made the most profound truths accessible to fishermen, shepherds, and farmers without diluting their power or depth. The crowds marveled, saying, "Never has a man spoken the way this man speaks" (John 7:46).

For every Christian who seeks to teach and evangelize effectively, simplicity and clarity are not optional—they are essential. Jesus' methods demonstrate that the goal of teaching is not to impress listeners with eloquence or intellect, but to impart understanding that leads to faith and obedience.

Avoiding Overload: The Value of Brevity

Jesus mastered the art of brevity. His sayings were concise, structured, and filled with eternal truth. The Sermon on the Mount, though among the most profound discourses ever delivered, can be read in about ten minutes. Yet within those brief words lie the principles of the Kingdom of Heaven, summarized in timeless expressions remembered for millennia.

Jesus avoided overwhelming His listeners with excessive information. He focused on essential truths and trusted His audience to reflect on and apply them. When He said, "You are the salt of the earth" (Matthew 5:13), He left space for reflection. The power of His brevity lay in its ability to invite meditation. Listeners were compelled to think, to explore, and to personalize what they had heard.

Human attention is limited, and the wise teacher understands that too much information can hinder learning. Jesus delivered truth in digestible portions.

He taught one principle at a time, using natural transitions and repetition to reinforce key ideas.

In contrast, the scribes and Pharisees buried truth beneath endless commentary and oral tradition. They turned divine revelation into a labyrinth of regulations that few could follow. Jesus, however, stripped away human additions, restoring the simple core of divine truth. His model reminds teachers today that less can often accomplish more. When God's truth is stated clearly, concisely, and with conviction, it penetrates the heart and endures in memory.

Jesus' Clear Communication in Everyday Language

Jesus' words were understandable to everyone because He spoke in the language of the people. He used familiar terms and relatable experiences to explain eternal truths. His teaching did not depend on abstract philosophy or technical vocabulary, but on clear, vivid expression that even a child could grasp.

He spoke of lamps, mustard seeds, lost sheep, bread, water, and treasure—things His audience encountered daily. Through these familiar images, He revealed spiritual realities. When He said, "I am the good shepherd," His listeners immediately understood the care, vigilance, and sacrifice implied in that image. When He declared, "The kingdom of heaven is like leaven," He connected invisible spiritual growth with the ordinary process of bread rising.

This clarity was intentional. Jesus wanted His hearers to understand, not merely admire, His words. His communication was rooted in empathy—He understood their world, their struggles, and their way of thinking. That understanding shaped how He taught.

Christian teachers must follow the same pattern. The goal is not to sound sophisticated but to make divine truth plain. A message that cannot be understood cannot be obeyed. Teaching must translate the eternal Word into language that speaks to the hearts of real people, living in real situations. The mark of a faithful teacher is not complexity, but clarity.

Speaking to Mixed Audiences Effectively

Jesus' audiences were often mixed—rich and poor, educated and uneducated, devout and indifferent, men and women, children and scholars. Yet His teaching reached them all without exclusion or compromise. He was equally effective in a synagogue among teachers of the Law and on a hillside surrounded by peasants.

How did He achieve such universality? First, He focused on the heart rather than intellectual status. Every human being, regardless of education or background, shares the same moral and spiritual needs: forgiveness, direction, and hope. Jesus' teaching addressed these universal realities.

Second, He used universal examples drawn from everyday life. A farmer scattering seed, a merchant seeking pearls, a father welcoming a lost son—these images spoke to every listener, regardless of social position. His parables allowed simple minds to grasp divine truth while challenging the learned to deeper reflection.

Third, He adjusted His tone and method according to the audience. With the proud, He confronted; with the humble, He comforted. With Nicodemus, He reasoned; with the Samaritan woman, He conversed; with the crowds, He illustrated. Yet the message remained consistent—salvation through faith, repentance, and obedience to the will of God.

The faithful teacher must also learn to adapt without compromising truth. Whether teaching a child or a theologian, clarity of purpose and compassion for the listener remain the same. The true test of teaching is not the impressiveness of delivery, but the depth of understanding it produces in every kind of listener.

Repeating for Emphasis and Memory

Jesus frequently repeated key truths to reinforce understanding. Repetition was one of His central teaching methods. When He said, "Truly, truly, I say to you," He emphasized the certainty and importance of what followed. When He repeated phrases such as "He who has ears to hear, let him hear," He called attention to the need for attentive listening and personal application.

Repetition in teaching is not redundancy—it is reinforcement. Every teacher knows that comprehension deepens through review. By repeating core truths in different contexts, Jesus ensured that His disciples would remember His words long after His ascension.

Consider how often Jesus spoke of faith, forgiveness, and the Kingdom. Each time, He approached the topic from a new angle, using different illustrations but always reinforcing the same truth. He used rhythm, parallelism, and repetition to anchor His message in the memory.

For instance, in Matthew 6:25–34, He repeated the command "Do not be anxious" three times, each with supporting illustrations from nature. By repetition, He calmed His disciples' hearts and engraved trust in God upon their minds.

Teachers who wish to follow Jesus' example must not fear repetition when it serves understanding. Repetition, when guided by purpose and variety, cements truth in the listener's heart. It transforms hearing into remembrance, and remembrance into conviction.

Simplicity as a Mark of Authority

The simplicity of Jesus' teaching did not lessen His authority—it confirmed it. The rabbis cloaked their teachings in complexity to project superiority, but Jesus' simplicity demonstrated divine confidence. Only one who possesses absolute truth can express it plainly. Those uncertain of their knowledge often hide behind complicated language, but Jesus' directness reflected His perfect mastery.

His simplicity commanded attention. When He said, "Let your statement be, 'Yes, yes' or 'No, no'" (Matthew 5:37), He demonstrated moral clarity that required no elaborate defense. His authority rested in truth itself, not in rhetorical flourish.

Moreover, simplicity reflected His purpose. He did not come to confuse, but to save. He said, "I thank You, Father, Lord of heaven and earth, that You have hidden these things from the wise and intelligent and have revealed them to infants" (Matthew 11:25). Divine wisdom reveals itself to the humble through simple truth.

The Christian teacher must emulate this authority born of simplicity. The power of God's Word lies not in how eloquently it is delivered, but in how faithfully it is communicated. The teacher who relies on Scripture, not sophistication, speaks with Christlike authority.

Cultivating Listener Understanding

The ultimate goal of teaching is not the transmission of words but the transformation of minds. Jesus always taught with the listener's understanding in view. He desired comprehension that led to conviction and conviction that led to obedience. "Everyone who hears these words of Mine and does them," He said, "will be like a wise man who built his house upon the rock" (Matthew 7:24).

Jesus cultivated understanding by engaging the mind, stirring the heart, and appealing to the will. He invited questions, encouraged reflection, and called for decision. His teaching was interactive—He expected His hearers to think, respond, and act.

He also recognized that understanding often unfolds gradually. He did not overwhelm His disciples with every truth at once but revealed it progressively as they were able to bear it (John 16:12). Effective teaching respects the learner's capacity and builds upon it patiently.

For the modern teacher, cultivating understanding means prioritizing clarity over complexity, explanation over display, and transformation over entertainment. The teacher must not merely deliver lessons but ensure comprehension through examples, review, and discussion.

When truth is understood, it produces obedience. When obedience matures, it bears fruit. Jesus' teaching, simple yet profound, produced disciples who would change the world. Simplicity and clarity, therefore, are not optional qualities—they are divine necessities for every teacher who follows in the steps of the Great Teacher.

Chapter 5: Teaching With Thought-Provoking Questions

Jesus Christ, the Great Teacher, often instructed not through long lectures or complicated arguments but through carefully crafted questions. His questions pierced hearts, challenged assumptions, and illuminated truth. In an age when rabbis sought prestige by giving answers to every inquiry, Jesus reversed expectations—He was the One who asked the questions that mattered most.

This approach reflected divine wisdom. A question invites reflection, while a statement demands reaction. Questions require the listener to engage both mind and conscience. They expose hidden motives, awaken self-awareness, and lead people to discover truth rather than merely receive it. Jesus did not use questions because He lacked knowledge; He used them to lead His hearers into self-examination and revelation.

His questions were instruments of grace and truth. To the complacent, they provoked conviction; to the humble, they stirred faith; to the hostile, they revealed hypocrisy. The Master's questions remain timeless—still capable of searching hearts and shaping disciples today. Every faithful teacher of God's Word must learn to ask questions that provoke thought, challenge belief, and lead the listener to encounter the truth personally.

The Power of Asking, Not Just Telling

Jesus often preferred to ask rather than to tell because He understood that self-discovery solidifies learning. When a person arrives at truth through reflection, it becomes deeply personal. Teaching by questioning transforms passive listeners into active participants.

Consider when Jesus asked His disciples, "Who do you say that I am?" (Matthew 16:15). He could have declared His identity directly, but instead, He led them to voice their conviction. Peter's confession—"You are the Christ, the Son of the living God"—was not merely an answer; it was a declaration of faith formed through reflection.

Questions engage the listener's reasoning and conscience. When Jesus asked, "For what will it profit a man if he gains the whole world and forfeits his soul?" (Matthew 16:26), He was not seeking information but awakening perspective. That single question continues to echo through history, confronting every person with the eternal value of the soul compared to temporary gain.

Jesus' method contrasts sharply with modern communication, which often prioritizes declaration over dialogue. While truth must be proclaimed, it must also be internalized. The teacher who asks well-designed questions becomes an instrument through whom the Holy Spirit exposes error and implants conviction. Questions create mental tension that only truth can resolve.

Teachers should learn from the Master to balance teaching and asking—to combine clear instruction with probing inquiry. Asking stimulates curiosity, opens dialogue, and invites repentance. It is a sacred tool for reaching both the mind and heart.

Guiding the Listener to Discovery

Jesus' questions were not random; they followed a divine pedagogy. He asked questions that guided listeners toward self-discovery. Rather than forcing belief, He allowed truth to unfold naturally within the heart. This process cultivated genuine conviction rather than mere agreement.

One vivid example is His conversation with the lawyer who sought to justify himself in Luke 10:25–37. The man asked, "Teacher, what shall I do to inherit eternal life?" Jesus replied, "What is written in the Law? How do you read it?" The question turned the inquirer back to the Scriptures and forced him to articulate the truth already present in the Word. The lawyer answered correctly, quoting Deuteronomy and Leviticus. But then Jesus asked another question through the parable of the Good Samaritan—"Which of these three do you think proved to be a neighbor?" (Luke 10:36).

Through questioning, Jesus led the man to confront his own prejudice and understand love as action, not theory. The lawyer discovered truth through guided reasoning, not mere instruction.

Teachers who guide learners to discovery help them take ownership of truth. When a person reaches an answer through reflection, the conviction is far stronger than if it were merely given. Guided discovery transforms knowledge into personal realization, producing obedience from the heart.

This technique demands patience and discernment. It requires listening carefully, asking questions at the right time, and allowing the listener to wrestle with the answer. When guided properly, the learner does not simply memorize truth—he encounters it.

Rhetorical Questions That Convict the Heart

Jesus often used rhetorical questions—questions that needed no verbal answer because the truth was self-evident. These questions pierced the conscience, bypassing intellectual defenses and striking directly at the heart.

For instance, when addressing His disciples' anxiety, Jesus asked, "Which of you by being anxious can add a single hour to his life?" (Matthew 6:27). The obvious answer—no one—forces the hearer to confront the futility of worry. A simple question accomplished what hours of explanation could not: it exposed the irrationality of fear and called for faith.

Rhetorical questions carry a unique moral force. They compel listeners to supply the answer internally, making the truth inescapable. When Jesus asked, "If you love those who love you, what reward do you have?" (Matthew 5:46), He revealed the hypocrisy of self-centered goodness and redefined love as selfless and divine.

These kinds of questions demand moral response. They awaken conscience, invite repentance, and force the listener to evaluate their heart before God. Unlike mere statements, rhetorical questions cannot be dismissed easily; they linger in the mind, continuing to challenge long after the conversation ends.

Teachers must learn to employ such questions wisely—not to shame or intimidate, but to stir reflection and conviction. The Word of God is living and active, and when framed in the form of a question, it penetrates deeply. As the Holy Spirit uses these questions, hearts are uncovered and truth takes root.

Questions That Reveal Motives

Jesus' questions often uncovered hidden motives. He had perfect knowledge of human hearts, yet He asked questions so that individuals would reveal their own intentions. This method allowed sinners to confront their true condition before God.

When the rich young ruler approached, asking, "What must I do to obtain eternal life?" (Matthew 19:16), Jesus responded with questions designed to expose his heart. After reviewing the commandments, Jesus asked him to sell his possessions and follow Him. The man's sadness revealed his true attachment. Jesus' questions drew out the idol within—the love of wealth—and forced self-recognition.

Similarly, when the disciples argued about who was greatest, Jesus asked, "What were you discussing on the way?" (Mark 9:33). Though He already knew, His question made them acknowledge their pride and silence themselves in shame. Through inquiry, He led them to humility.

These moments illustrate that spiritual growth begins with self-awareness. A good teacher helps learners recognize their inner motives before offering correction. Without confronting motives, instruction remains superficial.

In teaching and evangelism, questions that expose motives are invaluable. They bring sin into the open where it can be confessed and healed. For example, asking, "What is keeping you from fully trusting Christ?" may uncover barriers of pride, doubt, or misplaced priorities. Like Jesus, we must ask in love, not condemnation, seeking transformation rather than humiliation.

The purpose of motive-revealing questions is always redemption. Jesus' goal was never to embarrass but to enlighten. His questions led to repentance, healing, and renewed commitment to God.

Engaging the Hostile or the Skeptic

Jesus frequently faced hostile audiences—Pharisees who sought to trap Him, skeptics who demanded signs, and multitudes divided in belief. Yet even in confrontation, He maintained composure and responded with wisdom through questions that exposed hypocrisy and redirected the discussion toward truth.

When the Pharisees questioned His authority, asking, "By what authority are You doing these things?" (Matthew 21:23), Jesus replied with a counter-question: "The baptism of John, was it from heaven or from men?" (Matthew 21:25). His question silenced them, revealing their insincerity and fear of public opinion.

Jesus' questioning strategy in such encounters serves as a model for apologetics. Rather than reacting defensively, He redirected the issue to the heart of the matter. Questions turn attacks into opportunities for truth. They force opponents to evaluate their own reasoning and expose inconsistencies in their worldview.

To the Sadducees, who denied the resurrection, Jesus asked, "Have you not read what was spoken to you by God?" (Matthew 22:31). His question corrected both their ignorance of Scripture and their misunderstanding of divine power.

When engaging skeptics or hostile listeners, a teacher must imitate Jesus' calmness and discernment. A well-placed question can defuse hostility, clarify truth, and reveal hidden biases. The goal is not to win arguments but to win souls. The Christian teacher must respond to opposition with wisdom, gentleness, and Scripture-centered reasoning, using questions to guide others toward conviction rather than confrontation.

Questions That Deepen Discipleship

Jesus did not use questions only to challenge unbelievers; He also used them to deepen the faith of His disciples. His inquiries encouraged reflection, growth, and understanding. By asking, He trained them to think biblically, evaluate truth, and internalize His teachings.

When the storm threatened their boat, He asked, "Why are you afraid, you of little faith?" (Matthew 8:26). The question corrected and comforted simultaneously, reminding them that faith must triumph over fear. When they failed to understand His parables, He asked, "Do you not yet understand?"

(Matthew 15:16), prompting them to seek deeper comprehension.

Questions were central to Jesus' method of discipleship because they stimulated personal engagement. He was not producing mere followers but thinkers—believers who could discern truth, reason from Scripture, and teach others.

In John 21, after Peter's failure, Jesus restored him not with a sermon but with three questions: "Do you love Me?" Each repetition deepened Peter's reflection and renewed his devotion. That exchange demonstrates the power of questions to heal, recommission, and strengthen discipleship.

For modern teachers, this means that discipleship must be interactive. Teaching that invites dialogue and reflection produces mature believers. Asking, "What does this passage reveal about God's character?" or "How should this truth change your daily life?" moves learners from knowledge to obedience.

Discipleship deepens when believers wrestle with truth until it becomes conviction. Jesus' use of questions transformed followers into teachers and thinkers—men who would later stand before kings and proclaim the gospel with understanding and boldness.

Jesus' mastery of questioning reveals that divine teaching is not merely the delivery of answers but the awakening of the heart. The teacher who learns to ask as Jesus did can reach places in the human soul that mere explanation cannot touch. Questions that lead to discovery, conviction, and transformation are not human inventions—they are divine instruments shaped by truth and love.

Chapter 6: Teaching With Vivid Hyperbole

Among the many teaching methods Jesus Christ employed, one of the most striking and memorable was His use of hyperbole—intentional exaggeration for emphasis. In His perfect wisdom, Jesus knew that a statement magnified through vivid imagery could strike the conscience and linger in the mind long after the lesson was heard. Hyperbole, used under the guidance of divine purpose, was not deception but a tool for engraving moral truth upon the human heart.

Hyperbole in Jesus' teaching was never careless or comical. It served to awaken dull consciences, emphasize the seriousness of sin, and reveal the radical demands of righteousness. His listeners—accustomed to the teaching style of Jewish rabbis—recognized exaggeration as a legitimate and powerful rhetorical device. Yet Jesus' use of it was unique: it was moral, spiritual, and penetrating. His hyperboles were perfectly suited to His mission of confronting hypocrisy and calling men and women to wholehearted devotion to God.

For modern teachers of the Word, understanding how and why Jesus used vivid hyperbole guards against both extremes—flattening the meaning through over-literalism or distorting it through carelessness. Properly used, hyperbole adds force and clarity to instruction, capturing attention and driving the truth deep into the conscience.

The Role of Exaggeration in Jewish Teaching

In Jewish culture, hyperbole was a common and accepted method of teaching, particularly among prophets, sages, and rabbis. Hebrew expression often emphasized truth through contrast, symbol, or overstatement. This form of speech helped the teacher convey weighty concepts with brevity and memorability.

The Old Testament itself contains numerous examples. When Moses told Israel that their cities were "walled up to heaven" (Deuteronomy 1:28), he was not describing literal dimensions but expressing the formidable strength of Canaanite fortresses. Similarly, when David said, "All night I make my bed swim, I dissolve my couch with my tears" (Psalm 6:6), his words conveyed deep grief, not physical impossibility.

Jesus, as a Jewish teacher, employed this same linguistic tradition—but He did so with divine precision and purpose. His use of hyperbole revealed not exaggeration for effect alone, but exaggeration for transformation. Every overstatement in His speech was anchored in literal moral truth. The hyperbolic form served the spiritual function of magnifying the seriousness of His message.

In His Sermon on the Mount, for example, Jesus said, "If your right eye causes you to sin, tear it out and throw it from you" (Matthew 5:29). His Jewish audience understood that He was not commanding self-mutilation but illustrating the radical action required to avoid sin. By employing exaggeration, Jesus confronted moral complacency and underscored the urgency of repentance.

Hyperbole, therefore, was not rhetorical flourish—it was an inspired technique to cut through hardness of heart and awaken the moral imagination. It shocked listeners out of indifference and forced them to reckon with the absolute seriousness of God's standard.

Hyperbole to Emphasize Moral Truth

Jesus' use of hyperbole consistently pointed toward moral and spiritual realities. He magnified truth to clarify it, not to obscure it. His exaggerated statements carried literal implications, even when expressed in figurative form.

When He said, "It is easier for a camel to go through the eye of a needle than for a rich man to enter the kingdom of God" (Matthew 19:24), He was not referring to an actual gate in Jerusalem or a literal needle's eye. He was making a moral point: attachment to wealth can make salvation as impossible as a camel passing through a sewing needle's eye. The image shocks, but it clarifies the impossibility of divided loyalty.

Likewise, when He rebuked the Pharisees for straining out a gnat and swallowing a camel (Matthew 23:24), He used vivid exaggeration to expose hypocrisy—meticulous legalism in small matters alongside indifference to justice, mercy, and faithfulness. The absurdity of the image revealed the absurdity of their priorities.

Hyperbole functions as a moral magnifier. It takes what is easily ignored and enlarges it until it becomes impossible to overlook. Jesus used it to highlight sin's seriousness, hypocrisy's blindness, and righteousness's urgency. His exaggerated images became moral mirrors in which His listeners saw themselves clearly.

In the hands of the Great Teacher, hyperbole was a scalpel, not a club. It penetrated to the conscience without cruelty, bringing conviction rather than confusion. The exaggeration illuminated truth rather than distorting it, and its moral force continues to pierce hearts today.

Emotional Engagement Through Dramatization

Jesus' hyperboles were not only intellectually memorable but emotionally compelling. He dramatized truth to engage the whole person—mind, heart, and conscience. He knew that information alone rarely transforms; it must grip the emotions to produce repentance and faith.

When He said, "Why do you look at the speck that is in your brother's eye, but do not notice the log that is in your own?" (Matthew 7:3), the image was intentionally exaggerated and humorous. Yet behind the humor lay deep conviction. The absurdity of a man with a log protruding from his eye trying to remove a splinter from another's exposed the self-righteousness of judgmentalism. The exaggeration made the lesson unforgettable.

Similarly, His hyperbolic command to forgive "seventy times seven" times (Matthew 18:22) conveyed the boundless mercy expected of believers. The numbers were not meant to be counted literally but to express infinite forgiveness. The dramatization drew His listeners into the emotional core of divine compassion.

Hyperbole captures attention by creating surprise and contrast. It bypasses intellectual detachment and stirs feeling, making the hearer not only understand the truth but *feel* its weight. Jesus' words burned into memory because they appealed to imagination and emotion as well as intellect.

In Christian teaching today, this principle remains vital. Truth delivered without emotional force may be forgotten; truth dramatized appropriately becomes unforgettable. However, such dramatization must always serve Scripture's message, not personal theatrics. The teacher's goal is not to entertain but to awaken hearts to the gravity and glory of God's Word.

Avoiding Misinterpretation of Jesus' Intent

Because Jesus used vivid exaggeration, some have misinterpreted His words by taking figurative expressions literally or, conversely, dismissing literal doctrine as mere exaggeration. Both errors stem from a failure to interpret according to context and intent.

When Jesus said, "If anyone comes to Me and does not hate his father and mother... he cannot be My disciple" (Luke 14:26), He was not commanding hatred toward family but using hyperbole to emphasize supreme devotion to God. The exaggerated contrast reveals that loyalty to Christ must surpass all earthly attachments.

Misreading hyperbole can lead to distortion of doctrine or to unnecessary stumbling. Sound interpretation requires discernment—recognizing that Jesus' exaggerations communicated literal truths through figurative intensity. They were tools to clarify, not obscure, meaning.

The historical and literary context of each statement must be considered. The same Jesus who told us to pluck out an offending eye also healed the blind. The same One who said to hate family also commanded love for neighbor and enemy alike. Proper interpretation harmonizes all Scripture, recognizing hyperbole as a rhetorical form serving a literal moral reality.

Teachers of the Word must exercise care not to press Jesus' figurative speech into wooden literalism nor to explain away its moral force. Hyperbole was one of His sharpest instruments for awakening conscience. It must be respected as a means of divine persuasion rather than a puzzle to be softened or ignored.

Balancing Hyperbole With Literal Doctrine

Jesus never used hyperbole to replace literal doctrine but to reinforce it. The exaggeration emphasized, but the doctrine explained. Hyperbole makes truth memorable; doctrine makes it understandable.

For instance, when Jesus warned about removing the offending eye or hand to avoid sin, He dramatized the literal necessity of radical repentance. The moral command was clear: eliminate sin decisively, not half-heartedly. The hyperbole served the doctrine by heightening its seriousness.

When He said, "You cannot serve God and wealth" (Matthew 6:24), the absolute contrast underscored a literal spiritual truth—loyalty to Jehovah cannot coexist with idolatry. His exaggerated phrasing made the exclusive nature of devotion unmistakable.

Christian teachers must maintain this same balance. Hyperbole should never stand alone as teaching material; it must always direct the listener back to the literal truth it magnifies. The exaggerated form serves the factual foundation.

Balancing hyperbole with literal doctrine also prevents the teacher from lapsing into sensationalism. The goal is not to shock for its own sake but to enlighten the conscience. Every dramatic expression must ultimately drive the listener toward sound theology and obedient living. When properly balanced, hyperbole strengthens faith rather than confusing it.

Teaching Boldly with Reverence

Jesus' use of hyperbole exemplified bold teaching done with holy reverence. He never softened truth to avoid offense, yet He never used exaggeration carelessly. His words carried moral courage without theatrical excess. He spoke boldly because He spoke for God.

When He told His followers that it is better to lose a part of the body than to be cast into Gehenna (Matthew 5:29–30), His warning was severe yet reverent. The language was vivid, but the tone was sober. Hyperbole, in Jesus' hands, became a holy warning against the eternal consequences of sin.

Bold teaching demands this same reverence. To teach vividly is not to abandon seriousness but to communicate with the urgency that truth deserves. Teachers of the Word must learn to speak courageously—without apology when confronting sin, without hesitation when calling for repentance, and without compromise when declaring the exclusivity of salvation through Christ.

Yet even in boldness, reverence must govern tone and motive. Jesus' hyperbolic warnings were born of compassion, not condemnation. He dramatized judgment to save souls from it. His exaggerations were acts of mercy—divine attempts to awaken those in danger of eternal loss.

The teacher who follows Christ's example must likewise combine courage with humility, zeal with grace. To teach boldly with reverence is to let God's truth speak in full strength, clothed in holiness and love.

Jesus' use of vivid hyperbole reveals the beauty of divine communication—truth that stirs the imagination, engages emotion, and transforms the will. Every exaggeration in His teaching points to a greater reality: that the Kingdom of God demands total devotion, radical repentance, and undivided loyalty. When used with wisdom and reverence, hyperbole remains one of the teacher's most powerful tools to illuminate eternal truth in a darkened world.

Chapter 7: Teaching With Irrefutable Logic

Jesus Christ, the Great Teacher, was not only a master of compassion and illustration but also of logic and reason. His teaching was intellectually flawless, morally unassailable, and spiritually profound. He spoke with divine authority, but that authority was never arbitrary—it was grounded in truth communicated through sound reasoning. His use of logic was not human speculation; it was the perfect alignment of divine revelation with rational clarity.

Unlike the philosophers and religious leaders of His time, Jesus never argued for the sake of argument. His reasoning served redemptive purposes. Each syllogism, question, and analogy He used aimed to expose falsehood, defend righteousness, and lead His listeners to the truth of God's Word. His reasoning was not detached philosophy but applied theology—logic that compelled repentance, obedience, and faith.

In a world that increasingly separates emotion from intellect, Jesus remains the model of balanced communication—reason infused with love, clarity blended with conviction. He demonstrated that faith and logic are not adversaries but allies, both originating from the God of truth.

Jesus' Use of Cause-and-Effect Arguments

One of Jesus' most distinctive logical methods was His use of cause-and-effect reasoning. He often built arguments on observable principles that reflected spiritual truths, showing that the moral and natural worlds are governed by the same divine order. His listeners could verify His points through everyday experience.

In Matthew 7:17–18, He declared, "Every good tree bears good fruit, but the bad tree bears bad fruit. A good tree cannot produce bad fruit, nor can a bad tree produce good fruit." This is not only a moral statement but a logical one: cause determines effect, nature determines outcome. From this unassailable principle, Jesus drew a moral conclusion—true righteousness produces consistent behavior, while hypocrisy cannot yield holiness.

He used similar reasoning in Luke 6:39–40: "Can a blind man guide a blind man? Will they not both fall into a pit?" The cause-and-effect structure was evident—spiritual blindness in a teacher results in the downfall of his followers. This simple logic cut through religious pretense, revealing the peril of following leaders who themselves lack understanding.

By reasoning from the familiar to the eternal, Jesus demonstrated that divine truth is consistent with observable reality. His cause-and-effect arguments appealed both to intellect and conscience, affirming that obedience brings blessing while disobedience brings destruction. Such reasoning is irrefutable because it is rooted in both Scripture and common sense—the dual testimony of divine revelation and creation.

Logical Refutation of False Doctrine

Jesus' mastery of logic was most evident in His refutation of false doctrine. The religious leaders of His day—the Pharisees, Sadducees, and scribes—were experts in verbal manipulation and sophistry. Yet time and again, Jesus dismantled their arguments with flawless reasoning drawn directly from Scripture.

When the Sadducees denied the resurrection, they presented what they thought was an unanswerable dilemma: a woman who had seven husbands—whose wife would she be in the resurrection? (Matthew 22:23–28). Jesus' reply was logical, scriptural, and devastating. He exposed their false premise, saying, "You are mistaken, not understanding the Scriptures nor the power of God" (v. 29). He then reasoned from Exodus 3:6, where Jehovah declared, "I am the God of Abraham, and the God of Isaac, and the God of Jacob." The logical conclusion followed: God "is not the God of the dead but of the living" (v. 32). His argument refuted their error by appealing to grammar, context, and divine authority.

In John 10:34–36, when accused of blasphemy for calling Himself the Son of God, Jesus quoted Psalm 82:6 and applied sound reasoning: "If he called them gods, to whom the word of God came—and the Scripture cannot be broken—do you say of Him whom the Father sanctified and sent into the world, 'You are blaspheming,' because I said, 'I am the Son of God'?" His argument was impeccable: if Scripture applied a divine title to human judges, how much more appropriately could it apply to the divine Son.

Jesus' logic was never abstract. He used it to protect the integrity of Scripture and to expose false teachers. His reasoning was irrefutable because it was inseparable from the Word of God. For those who love truth, His logic illuminated; for those who resisted, it condemned.

Every teacher who defends the faith must learn this holy reasoning. The Scriptures themselves provide not only revelation but also the framework of sound logic. When teachers reason biblically, their defense of truth becomes unassailable—not through human cleverness, but through divine coherence.

Clear Deductive Reasoning in Parables

Jesus' parables were not only illustrations; they were exercises in deductive logic. Through simple stories, He led listeners from concrete examples to spiritual conclusions, following patterns of reasoning that were clear, consistent, and compelling.

In the Parable of the Wise and Foolish Builders (Matthew 7:24–27), Jesus presented two cases—one man who built on rock, another on sand. The deductive logic is evident:

1. Both hear His words.
2. One obeys, one ignores.
3. One stands firm, one collapses. **Therefore:** obedience to Christ's teaching is the only foundation that endures.

Each parable contains a premise, observation, and conclusion. In the Parable of the Lost Sheep (Luke

15:3–7), Jesus reasons from human compassion to divine mercy: if a shepherd rejoices over one lost sheep recovered, how much more does God rejoice over one sinner who repents? The argument is not emotional alone—it is logically sound, moving from the lesser to the greater (*a fortiori* reasoning).

His parables often followed the structure of analogy-based deduction—using the familiar to reason toward the unseen. The Parable of the Sower (Matthew 13:3–9) logically distinguishes between external exposure to truth and internal receptivity, illustrating that the heart's condition determines fruitfulness.

Jesus' logical use of parables demonstrates that truth can be both accessible and intellectually rigorous. He never asked His hearers to abandon reason but to purify it—to reason rightly, in submission to revelation.

For modern teachers, His example underscores the importance of clear structure and logical flow in presenting biblical truth. Parables and illustrations must not replace reasoning but serve it—helping listeners trace the divine logic from truth to application.

Challenging Pharisaic Legalism

Nowhere did Jesus' logic shine more brightly than in His confrontation with Pharisaic legalism. Their teachings distorted divine law into a maze of traditions, contradictions, and man-made regulations. Jesus exposed their inconsistencies through piercing logic that left them speechless.

In Matthew 12:9–12, when accused of breaking the Sabbath by healing a man's hand, Jesus reasoned from their own practices: "What man is there among you who has a sheep, and if it falls into a pit on the Sabbath, will he not take hold of it and lift it out? How much more valuable then is a man than a sheep!" His argument was impeccable: if compassion for an animal was permitted on the Sabbath, compassion for a human being must be even more lawful.

Similarly, when the Pharisees condemned His disciples for plucking grain on the Sabbath (Matthew 12:1–8), Jesus appealed to Scripture and logic simultaneously. He cited David eating the consecrated bread and the priests working on the Sabbath—both technically breaking the law yet guiltless. His reasoning revealed that mercy and purpose outweigh ritualism. The conclusion was undeniable: "The Son of Man is Lord of the Sabbath."

Pharisaic logic was circular, self-serving, and inconsistent. Jesus' logic was linear, transparent, and anchored in divine purpose. He did not reject the Law but restored its rightful meaning. His reasoning always led back to the heart of God—a balance of truth and mercy.

Today, teachers must follow Christ's example in challenging man-made traditions that obscure God's truth. Logical reasoning grounded in Scripture can dismantle false systems and restore the purity of divine instruction.

Bringing Listeners to the Truth

Jesus' logical arguments were never cold or purely intellectual. His reasoning always aimed to bring listeners to personal truth—to confront them with reality and compel decision. Logic in His teaching was not an end in itself but a means to transformation.

When He asked, "Which of you convicts Me of sin?" (John 8:46), His question was not rhetorical bravado but moral reasoning. The silence of His accusers confirmed His innocence, proving His divine authority. Logic here served moral revelation.

When reasoning with His disciples, Jesus often used logical progression to strengthen faith. In

Matthew 6:25–30, He reasoned from lesser to greater—if God feeds the birds and clothes the lilies, how much more will He care for His children? The argument was simple, consistent, and persuasive. It led not to mere assent but to trust.

His goal was always illumination leading to transformation. The mind engaged through logic; the heart moved through conviction. Together they produced obedience. True teaching must follow this same pattern—logic that leads to life.

When teachers present truth logically, they reflect the nature of God Himself. The Creator is orderly, consistent, and rational. Biblical teaching that mirrors His order honors both faith and reason.

Modeling Logic with Humility

Jesus' flawless reasoning was always tempered with humility. He never used logic to humiliate or dominate but to enlighten and redeem. His debates were not displays of intellectual superiority but expressions of divine compassion. Even when silencing His opponents, His purpose was correction, not conquest.

In John 3, Jesus reasoned gently with Nicodemus, explaining spiritual rebirth through logical analogy: "That which is born of the flesh is flesh, and that which is born of the Spirit is spirit" (v. 6). His logic was precise yet patient, inviting Nicodemus to understanding rather than forcing it.

In John 8, His reasoning exposed hypocrisy—"He who is without sin among you, let him be the first to throw a stone" (v. 7)—yet He followed it with mercy: "Neither do I condemn you; go and sin no more" (v. 11). His logic was powerful but never cruel.

This union of truth and humility is the mark of divine teaching. A teacher who reasons without humility may win arguments but lose souls. Jesus demonstrated that sound reasoning and gentle spirit must walk hand in hand. Logic without love hardens; love without logic misleads.

Teachers today must therefore model reasoning with grace—clear in argument, firm in truth, but humble in tone. Our goal, like the Master's, is not intellectual victory but spiritual awakening.

Jesus' use of irrefutable logic proves that divine truth is both rational and revelatory. His reasoning was consistent with Scripture, creation, and conscience, showing that faith never contradicts reason but fulfills it. The Teacher who is Truth Himself demonstrated that to love God with all one's mind is as vital as loving Him with heart and soul.

Those who teach the Word of God must therefore learn to reason as Jesus did—accurately, persuasively, and humbly. For in Christ's logical teaching we see the perfect marriage of divine wisdom and human understanding, a model for all who desire to bring others from confusion to conviction and from darkness to light.

Chapter 8: Teaching With Parables That Reveal and Conceal

No teaching method of Jesus Christ has captured the hearts and minds of believers more than His use of parables. These brief, vivid stories communicated eternal truths in ways that were simple yet profound, familiar yet deeply spiritual. Through parables, Jesus bridged the gap between the natural and the divine, using everyday scenes to reveal the mysteries of the Kingdom of God. Yet, His parables also served a dual function—they simultaneously *revealed* truth to those who were humble and teachable and *concealed* it from those who were proud and hardened.

This deliberate duality demonstrates the divine wisdom of the Master Teacher. Jesus' parables were not simply illustrations meant to entertain; they were instruments of spiritual discernment. They sifted listeners according to their heart condition, dividing those who truly sought truth from those who merely sought spectacle. In Matthew 13, Jesus explained this purpose clearly to His disciples, affirming that the ability to understand His parables was a privilege granted by Jehovah to those who responded in faith.

The parables remain among the most powerful teaching tools in the Church's possession. They remind us that divine truth is not for the indifferent but for those who hunger and thirst for righteousness. Every parable invites reflection, self-examination, and decision.

The Purpose of Parables (Matthew 13)

Matthew 13 stands as the central chapter on Jesus' use of parables. It begins with the Parable of the Sower and unfolds into a series of seven parables that collectively describe the mysteries of the Kingdom. When His disciples asked, "Why do You speak to them in parables?" Jesus answered:

"To you it has been granted to know the mysteries of the kingdom of heaven, but to them it has not been granted" (Matthew 13:11).

This statement reveals the divine intention behind parabolic teaching—it is both *revelatory* and *restrictive*. The parables were not designed to make truth obscure, but to protect it from those who approached it with hardened hearts and unbelieving minds. They revealed truth to those with spiritual perception and concealed it from those who rejected light.

Jesus explained that His use of parables fulfilled the spiritual law of receptivity: those who respond to light receive more, while those who reject it lose even the light they once had. "For whoever has, to him more shall be given, and he will have an abundance; but whoever does not have, even what he has shall be taken away from him" (v. 12).

Thus, parables are instruments of divine justice as well as mercy. They reward humility and punish hardness. They separate genuine disciples from superficial hearers. Through parables, Jesus unveiled the hidden nature of the Kingdom—its growth, opposition, value, and final judgment—while concealing it from those unwilling to repent.

The purpose of parables, then, is not to make God's truth complicated, but to make it selective. Only those willing to hear with faith and obedience will grasp their meaning.

Parables as Tests of Heart Condition

Each parable Jesus told served as a mirror reflecting the listener's heart. The Parable of the Sower (Matthew 13:3–9, 18–23) especially demonstrates this function. The same seed—the Word of God—was sown in every place, but the results varied depending on the soil, which symbolized the heart.

The hardened path represented the hearer who rejected the Word outright. The rocky soil pictured the shallow hearer who received with emotion but lacked endurance. The thorny ground symbolized the double-minded hearer, choked by worldly cares and wealth. Only the good soil—honest, humble, and receptive—produced fruit in abundance.

Through this parable, Jesus defined His own teaching ministry. The effectiveness of divine truth depends not on the skill of the teacher or the clarity of the Word, but on the condition of the listener's heart. The parable tested whether the hearer would respond with repentance and faith or remain indifferent and unfruitful.

Every subsequent parable follows this principle. The Parable of the Ten Virgins tests readiness; the Parable of the Talents tests stewardship; the Parable of the Two Sons tests obedience. Each story demands moral evaluation and spiritual response.

The modern Church must recover this dimension of parabolic teaching. Too often, parables are treated as gentle illustrations rather than spiritual tests. Jesus' parables confronted listeners with moral decision—they could not remain neutral. Likewise, when the Word of God is taught faithfully today, it still separates the teachable from the proud, the obedient from the rebellious.

Fulfillment of Prophetic Teaching Method

Jesus' use of parables was not a new innovation but the fulfillment of an ancient prophetic tradition. Matthew 13:34–35 declares, "All these things Jesus spoke to the crowds in parables... so that what was spoken through the prophet might be fulfilled: 'I will open My mouth in parables; I will utter things hidden since the foundation of the world.'"

This quotation from Psalm 78:2 refers to the teaching ministry of Asaph, who used historical parables to reveal divine lessons from Israel's past. Jesus fulfilled this pattern perfectly, unveiling the mysteries of God's redemptive plan through story and symbol.

The prophets had often used symbolic narratives to communicate divine truth—the vineyard of Isaiah 5, the potter's vessel in Jeremiah 18, and Ezekiel's acted parables. Jesus stood in this prophetic line but brought it to its highest point. His parables were not merely symbolic warnings; they were revelations of the hidden Kingdom.

The phrase "things hidden since the foundation of the world" indicates that the parables unveiled truths previously concealed in the Old Testament—the spiritual nature of the Kingdom, the rejection of the Messiah, the mixture of true and false believers, and the final separation at judgment.

Thus, the parables of Jesus were not random moral stories but prophetic revelations. They disclosed the very structure of God's kingdom program—its inception, growth, opposition, and consummation. Through them, Jesus bridged prophecy and fulfillment, revealing God's eternal purposes through earthly pictures.

Separating Truth-Seekers From the Hardened

One of the most sobering functions of Jesus' parables was their ability to separate truth-seekers from those hardened in unbelief. In Matthew 13:14–15, Jesus quoted Isaiah 6:9–10 to explain that His parables fulfilled the prophecy of spiritual blindness:

"You will keep on hearing, but will not understand; you will keep on seeing, but will not perceive; for the heart of this people has become dull."

This was not an arbitrary withholding of truth but a judicial consequence of persistent rejection.

Those who repeatedly refused light were left in darkness. The parables thus became both revelation and retribution—they illuminated the obedient and confounded the obstinate.

The same Word that softens one heart hardens another, depending on the hearer's response. This principle operates throughout Scripture. Pharaoh's heart was hardened by repeated rejection of God's commands. In the same way, those who heard Jesus' words without repentance became increasingly blind.

Yet even this concealment was merciful. By veiling the full weight of truth, Jesus spared hardened hearers from greater condemnation. As He later said, "That slave who knew his master's will and did not get ready or act in accord with his will, will receive many lashes" (Luke 12:47). The parables concealed judgment from those unwilling to bear it.

The dividing effect of parables continues today. When Scripture is taught faithfully, some receive it with joy and transformation, while others dismiss it with apathy or hostility. The parable remains a test of the heart—a spiritual filter revealing who truly belongs to the Kingdom.

Jesus' Explanations to His Disciples

While Jesus often left the crowds with unexplained parables, He always provided private explanations to His disciples. This demonstrates that spiritual understanding is granted through divine illumination to those who follow Him closely.

In Matthew 13:36–43, Jesus explained the Parable of the Wheat and the Weeds. He identified each element: the sower as the Son of Man, the field as the world, the good seed as the sons of the Kingdom, and the tares as the sons of the wicked one. His clear explanation shows that parables are not mystical riddles but vehicles of truth to those enlightened by faith.

The disciples' privileged understanding fulfilled the principle Jesus had stated earlier: "To you it has been granted to know the mysteries of the kingdom of heaven" (v. 11). This divine granting did not result from superior intellect but from obedient discipleship. They sought the meaning of His words, and in seeking, they found.

Jesus' private explanations also modeled how teachers should guide learners. He demonstrated patience, precision, and completeness. He interpreted every symbol and clarified every connection, leaving no ambiguity for those who truly wanted to understand.

In this, Jesus revealed the relational nature of revelation. Truth is not given to the curious but to the committed. Understanding grows in proportion to faithfulness. Teachers who follow Christ's example will nurture this same relationship between truth and obedience, ensuring that those who hear may also comprehend and apply.

Application of Parables in Modern Evangelism

The parables of Jesus remain timeless models for teaching and evangelism. They appeal to universal human experience, transcending culture and time. Their enduring power lies in their ability to awaken conscience and call for moral and spiritual decision.

In evangelism, parables can open conversations with those who might resist direct preaching. Their indirect approach invites reflection without immediate defensiveness. For example, when explaining repentance, a teacher might begin with the Parable of the Prodigal Son—allowing the hearer to see himself in the story before confronting him with personal application.

Parables also teach that evangelism is not about intellectual persuasion alone but about preparing hearts to receive truth. The Parable of the Sower reminds us that only the Spirit of God can make the seed fruitful. Teachers and evangelists must sow faithfully, trusting Jehovah to bring the increase.

Moreover, parables illustrate the importance of clarity and relatability in communication. Jesus chose familiar, concrete imagery—farming, fishing, family life—to express unseen realities. Modern teachers should follow this same model, using examples from everyday life to reveal divine truth without compromising doctrine.

Finally, parables remind us that not every listener will respond positively. Some will reject truth despite clear explanation. Yet like the Sower, we must continue to sow, confident that some hearts will produce fruit a hundredfold.

Through parables that reveal and conceal, Jesus taught that understanding truth is not merely a matter of intellect but of heart condition. In evangelism and teaching, our task is to follow His example—speaking clearly, wisely, and compassionately—trusting God to open the ears and hearts of those who truly seek Him.

Chapter 9: Parables With Selective Detail for Maximum Effect

Jesus Christ, the Great Teacher, demonstrated not only divine wisdom in what He said but divine restraint in what He chose not to say. His parables stand as masterpieces of selective communication—stories rich in meaning, yet remarkably concise. He included only what was necessary to illuminate the moral and spiritual principle at hand. Every word, image, and character served a precise function. This selective economy of detail gave His parables enduring clarity, emotional power, and universal accessibility.

The genius of Jesus' storytelling was not in elaborate description but in perfect proportion. He told stories that were brief enough to remember, simple enough to grasp, and profound enough to meditate upon for a lifetime. He never overloaded His listeners with unnecessary information. Instead, He provided just enough context to direct their attention toward the spiritual truth being revealed.

In this restraint, Jesus taught an essential principle for every teacher of God's Word: clarity requires selection. Truth is often best understood not when everything is said, but when only what *must* be said is emphasized. The power of teaching lies as much in what is left out as in what is spoken.

The Art of Teaching With Necessary Detail

Every parable of Jesus contains exactly what the message requires—no more, no less. He included only what was essential to communicate divine truth. This economy of expression ensured that His teaching was memorable and undistracted by superfluous elements.

For example, in the Parable of the Good Samaritan (Luke 10:30–37), Jesus described a man traveling from Jerusalem to Jericho, attacked by robbers, stripped, and left half-dead. He then introduced three characters—a priest, a Levite, and a Samaritan. Each detail serves the story's purpose: to expose hypocrisy and redefine the meaning of neighborly love. Jesus did not explain the robber's motives, the man's identity, or the Samaritan's background. These omissions sharpened the focus on compassion rather than curiosity.

Similarly, in the Parable of the Lost Sheep (Luke 15:3–7), Jesus mentioned a shepherd with one hundred sheep, one lost, and ninety-nine left behind. He offered no information about the terrain, weather, or time of day. The listener's attention was fixed on one idea: the shepherd's relentless love for the lost.

This restraint reveals divine teaching artistry. Jesus knew that unnecessary detail dilutes impact. Every teacher of Scripture must learn this discipline. When teaching, one must discern which facts serve the message and which distract from it. The goal is not exhaustive explanation but focused illumination.

Teaching with necessary detail honors both truth and listener. It respects the Word of God by emphasizing its central point and respects the audience by not overwhelming them with information that clouds comprehension.

Highlighting Truth Through Simplicity

Jesus' restraint in detail created simplicity, and simplicity amplified truth. His parables are never cluttered with digressions or ornamental language. They strike directly at the heart with clarity and moral force.

The Parable of the Prodigal Son (Luke 15:11–32) illustrates this principle beautifully. Jesus provided only what was essential for the listener to understand the son's rebellion, repentance, and restoration. He did not describe the far country, the farm, or the father's household in elaborate terms. The story's power lies in its moral contrast—sin and grace, rebellion and forgiveness, pride and humility.

Simplicity is not weakness but strength. The more concise the story, the more powerful its truth becomes. The absence of unnecessary detail invites the listener to engage imagination and conscience. The mind fills in the background, and the heart absorbs the message.

In teaching, verbosity often clouds truth. Jesus' example shows that simplicity clarifies, focuses, and transforms. As Ecclesiastes 12:10 says, "The Teacher sought to find delightful words and to write words of truth correctly." Jesus' words were delightful not for their complexity but for their purity.

The Christian teacher must emulate this simplicity—choosing clarity over complexity, essentials over embellishment, and truth over trivia. To teach with simplicity is to magnify the Word of God without overshadowing it.

Avoiding Over-Explanation

Jesus never over-explained His parables. He trusted His listeners to think, reflect, and draw conclusions. Over-explanation can rob a listener of discovery, while under-guidance can lead to confusion. Jesus achieved perfect balance—He said enough to guide, but not so much as to smother insight.

When He told the Parable of the Sower, He explained it only to His disciples, not the multitudes (Matthew 13:10–23). He knew that understanding required spiritual hunger. To the casual hearer, additional explanation would not produce faith. To the sincere disciple, a brief clarification would deepen understanding. His restraint revealed both discernment and dependence upon the Holy Spirit's illuminating work.

Over-explanation can also weaken conviction. A truth that is dissected excessively becomes an intellectual exercise rather than a moral challenge. Jesus' parables demanded participation; the hearer had to think, feel, and respond. When the teacher provides all the answers, the listener is deprived of spiritual wrestling. Jesus left intentional tension in His stories to provoke meditation.

For instance, in the Parable of the Workers in the Vineyard (Matthew 20:1–16), the landowner's actions appear unfair to human logic. Jesus did not resolve the tension by giving an exhaustive theological explanation. Instead, He left His audience to grapple with divine justice and grace. The power of the parable lies in its unanswered questions.

Teachers must resist the impulse to over-explain every nuance. God's truth is clear, but its application must be personally embraced. The teacher's task is to illuminate, not to dominate the listener's understanding. Jesus trusted the Word of God to work in receptive hearts without exhaustive elaboration—and so should we.

Emphasizing Moral Lessons Over Narratives

In every parable, the story serves the message, never the other way around. Jesus did not tell stories for entertainment but for moral instruction. The narrative was merely the vessel; the truth was the treasure.

For example, in the Parable of the Rich Fool (Luke 12:16–21), Jesus offered a concise story: a wealthy man hoarded his harvest and planned for self-indulgence, only to die that very night. The story contains minimal detail, yet its moral is unmistakable—greed blinds the soul to eternal realities. The brevity of the narrative directs all focus toward the warning: "So is the one who stores up treasure for himself, and is not rich toward God."

Likewise, in the Parable of the Ten Virgins (Matthew 25:1–13), the simplicity of the story reinforces the moral lesson—spiritual preparedness. Jesus avoided unnecessary explanation about the customs of marriage or the personalities of the virgins. Every element existed to communicate one principle: be ready for the coming of the Bridegroom.

This focus teaches that Scripture is not about satisfying curiosity but transforming character. Stories that captivate the imagination but fail to convict the conscience miss the purpose of divine teaching. Jesus never entertained; He enlightened. His parables called for repentance, faith, and obedience.

Teachers of God's Word must keep this priority. The moral lesson must always take precedence over the narrative appeal. Details exist only to serve doctrine, not distract from it. Teaching that entertains but does not convict betrays the example of the Master.

Jesus' Strategic Use of Gaps

One of the most brilliant features of Jesus' teaching was His strategic use of *gaps*—deliberate omissions that forced listeners to think. These narrative gaps invited meditation and self-application. What Jesus left unsaid was often as significant as what He spoke.

Consider the Parable of the Older Brother in the story of the Prodigal Son. The narrative ends abruptly with the father pleading for reconciliation, yet the older brother's response is never revealed. This unfinished conclusion confronts the listener: *What will you do? Will you rejoice over grace or resent it?* The gap transforms the story from a mere lesson into a personal challenge.

Another example is the Parable of the Unforgiving Servant (Matthew 18:23–35). The story concludes with the servant being handed over to the torturers, but Jesus does not describe what happened next. The silence invites reflection on the seriousness of unforgiveness.

These gaps stimulate self-examination. By leaving the conclusion open, Jesus invited His audience to complete the story within their own conscience. He trusted them to apply truth personally under the Spirit's conviction.

Modern teachers should use this technique with care. When everything is explained, nothing is discovered. When too little is said, confusion arises. But when a gap is left intentionally for reflection, truth penetrates deeply. Silence, properly timed, can be as instructive as speech.

Teaching With Precision

The precision of Jesus' parables reflects divine perfection. Every word was chosen with purpose; every omission was deliberate. His speech was as economical as it was powerful. Precision ensured that His message remained clear, memorable, and authoritative.

In the Parable of the Mustard Seed (Matthew 13:31–32), Jesus condensed an immense truth into two verses. The image of a small seed growing into a tree captured the expansion of God's Kingdom from humble beginnings to global influence. No unnecessary detail was added—only what would permanently anchor the concept in the hearer's mind.

Precision was not cold exactness but focused truthfulness. Jesus spoke with such accuracy that no word could be removed without loss or added without confusion. His parables carried perfect balance—enough information to instruct, but never enough to distract.

For Christian teachers, this is the highest standard. Precision requires preparation, discipline, and reverence for the Word of God. Each statement must be weighed for clarity and faithfulness to Scripture. Vagueness weakens authority; precision strengthens it.

The teacher who follows Christ's model will learn to speak with accuracy and restraint—avoiding exaggeration that distorts, verbosity that dulls, or carelessness that confuses. To teach with precision is to imitate the Great Teacher, whose every word carried eternal weight and flawless purpose.

Jesus' parables demonstrate that divine truth requires both selection and simplicity. By including only essential details, He ensured that His words penetrated the heart rather than merely pleasing the ear. His strategic restraint in detail was not minimalism—it was mastery. Every silence was intentional, every word exact, every lesson unforgettable.

To teach as Jesus taught is to embrace this divine economy of expression—to speak with purpose, highlight what matters most, and trust the Spirit to illuminate truth in the hearts of those who hear.

Chapter 10: Parables From Everyday Life

Jesus Christ, the Great Teacher, reached the minds and hearts of His listeners through the everyday experiences that shaped their lives. He took the common and revealed the eternal; He transformed ordinary objects and daily routines into windows through which people could see divine truth. His parables were not abstract theological lectures—they were drawn from the fields, the seas, the homes, and the streets of real life.

By grounding His teaching in the familiar, Jesus made truth accessible to all. Farmers, fishermen, craftsmen, merchants, and homemakers could all understand His lessons because He spoke their language. His examples were not contrived but genuine, reflecting both the natural world and the moral order that Jehovah had built into creation. Through these relatable images, Jesus communicated timeless principles of faith, obedience, love, and discipleship.

This approach reflects divine wisdom in communication: to reach the heart, truth must be relatable; to change lives, truth must be remembered.

Jesus' parables endure because they speak as clearly to the modern laborer and teacher as they did to the ancient fisherman and farmer. In His teaching, we see that the world itself is a classroom, and every act of daily life can reflect the truths of God's Kingdom.

Farming, Fishing, and Family Scenes

Jesus frequently drew His lessons from the three main arenas of first-century Jewish life—agriculture, fishing, and family. These images formed the backbone of His parabolic teaching because they were instantly recognizable to His audience.

Agricultural imagery filled many of His parables. The Sower (Matthew 13:3–9), the Wheat and the Weeds (Matthew 13:24–30), the Mustard Seed (Matthew 13:31–32), and the Vine and the Branches (John 15:1–8) all speak the language of farming. Each image revealed spiritual principles about growth, fruitfulness, and divine care. The soil represented hearts, the seed symbolized the Word, and the harvest depicted the outcome of faith.

Fishing imagery was equally familiar. Jesus called His disciples from the shores of Galilee, saying, "Follow Me, and I will make you fishers of men" (Matthew 4:19). He spoke of dragnets (Matthew

13:47–50) and the sorting of fish to illustrate divine judgment and separation between the righteous and the wicked. His mastery of such images reflected His understanding of human labor and the discipline it required.

Family scenes appeared often in His teaching—the Lost Son, the Two Brothers, the Unforgiving Servant, the Wise and Foolish Builders. These parables drew on household life to illustrate forgiveness, stewardship, authority, and relationship. Listeners saw themselves reflected in fathers, sons, servants, and stewards.

By using the familiar, Jesus made the eternal personal. He did not speak down to His listeners but met them where they lived, inviting them to find divine meaning in the ordinary.

Teaching in Familiar Terms

Jesus' use of familiar language reflected His compassion and perfect teaching wisdom. He understood that profound truth, when expressed in simple terms, becomes accessible to all. His teaching was never an exercise in intellectual superiority but an act of divine accommodation—truth translated into the language of human experience.

When Jesus spoke of the Kingdom of Heaven, He compared it to things His audience could see and touch: a mustard seed, yeast, treasure hidden in a field, or a pearl of great value. Each image was drawn from daily observation, yet each revealed eternal reality.

This method reflects a principle of revelation found throughout Scripture: God speaks in ways that humans can understand. From the creation narrative to the teachings of the prophets, divine truth is expressed through human experience. Jesus, as the incarnate Word, perfected this communication by embodying truth and expressing it through earthly language.

By teaching in familiar terms, Jesus dismantled barriers to understanding. He did not rely on obscure symbolism or complex philosophical reasoning. Instead, He invited His listeners into reflection through what they already knew. Familiarity bred not contempt, but conviction.

For today's teachers, this principle is essential. The truth of Scripture must never be buried under theological jargon or abstract theory. When truth is clothed in everyday language, it becomes memorable and transformative. Teachers who follow Jesus' model will speak plainly, illustrating divine principles through the language of real life.

Anchoring Truth in Daily Experience

Jesus not only used familiar language—He anchored truth in daily experience. His parables often turned everyday actions into moral and spiritual metaphors. This approach made His teaching impossible to forget. Every time a farmer sowed seed or a woman kneaded dough, the parable came alive again.

For example, in the Parable of the Leaven (Matthew 13:33), Jesus likened the Kingdom of Heaven to yeast that a woman hid in flour until it permeated the whole batch. The image illustrated the quiet yet pervasive influence of divine truth in the world and in the heart. Every woman who baked bread afterward carried a living reminder of the Kingdom's silent power.

In the Parable of the Lamp (Matthew 5:14–16), Jesus connected a universal household task—lighting a lamp—to a spiritual calling: "You are the light of the world." Every evening when His listeners lit their homes, they were reminded of their responsibility to reflect God's light through righteous living.

This method transformed routine into revelation. Jesus demonstrated that truth is not confined to temples or synagogues—it is woven into the fabric of life. The plow, the net, the vineyard, and the home all became instruments of instruction.

Anchoring truth in daily experience teaches that divine principles are not abstract ideals but practical realities. Every believer can live out the truths Jesus taught, finding opportunities in work, family, and community to demonstrate Kingdom values.

How Jesus Used Work and Labor as Metaphors

Work and labor were central to Jesus' teaching. He dignified ordinary occupations by using them as metaphors for discipleship and service. Through this, He taught that spiritual growth and faithfulness require the same perseverance, discipline, and diligence that honest work demands.

In the Parable of the Workers in the Vineyard (Matthew 20:1–16), Jesus illustrated divine generosity through the payment of laborers. The vineyard represented God's Kingdom, the workers His servants, and the wages His gracious rewards. The parable highlighted the sovereignty of God in dispensing grace while affirming the dignity of service.

In John 9:4, Jesus declared, "We must work the works of Him who sent Me as long as it is day; night is coming when no one can work." Here He connected the urgency of spiritual labor with the temporal limits of human life. Just as farmers must sow within the season, believers must serve within their allotted time.

Even His calling of fishermen reflected this theology of labor. Fishing required patience, teamwork, and endurance—qualities essential for evangelism. By transforming fishermen into apostles, Jesus demonstrated that ordinary work can become extraordinary ministry when done for the glory of God.

Jesus' use of labor imagery elevates daily work from drudgery to discipleship. It teaches that faith is not confined to moments of worship but expressed through the faithful performance of every task, however small.

Discipleship and Cost Illustrated Through Daily Tasks

Many of Jesus' parables also used daily activities to illustrate the cost and discipline of discipleship. He used the simplicity of work to convey the seriousness of commitment.

In Luke 9:62, He declared, "No one who puts his hand to the plow and looks back is fit for the kingdom of God." The plowman's focus became a symbol of spiritual perseverance. Discipleship demands forward motion, not divided loyalty. The image of plowing—a task known to every farmer—made the lesson unforgettable.

Likewise, in Luke 14:28–30, Jesus used the example of a builder who counts the cost before constructing a tower. The illustration, drawn from common experience, conveyed the necessity of deliberate commitment in following Him. Discipleship, like construction, requires planning, endurance, and sacrifice.

The Parable of the Talents (Matthew 25:14–30) employed the work of servants to depict responsibility in spiritual service. The servants' labor reflected faithfulness and accountability—principles every believer must embody.

Through these everyday metaphors, Jesus made discipleship practical. He taught that faith is not theoretical but lived out in obedience, perseverance, and stewardship. His listeners understood that following Him would require the same diligence they already practiced in their daily labor—but with eternal stakes.

Everyday Parables for the Modern Pulpit

The same approach Jesus used remains vital for teachers and preachers today. Modern audiences, like ancient ones, respond most deeply when truth connects with life. The preacher who fills sermons with relatable examples—drawn from work, family, and creation—follows in the steps of the Master.

However, these examples must be faithful to Scripture, not mere illustrations for entertainment. The goal is to illuminate God's truth through life, not to replace it with anecdotes. Jesus' parables were effective not because they were clever but because they were truthful and purposeful.

In today's world of complexity and distraction, everyday parables remain powerful. A teacher can draw upon modern equivalents of farming, fishing, and household life—fields replaced by offices, nets replaced by networks, households replaced by digital communities—without losing the timeless principles. Truth expressed through familiar experiences still reaches hearts.

Moreover, this approach reinforces the integration of faith and life. Christianity is not confined to sacred spaces; it permeates every sphere of daily existence. Teachers who follow Jesus' model will help believers see the divine in the ordinary, transforming work, family, and community into opportunities for worship and witness.

Jesus' everyday parables remind us that God's truth is not distant—it walks among us, works beside us, and speaks through the rhythms of life. When we teach as He taught, we awaken hearts to the reality that every moment, every task, and every encounter can reveal the glory of God.

Chapter 11: Parables From God's Creation

Jesus Christ, the Great Teacher, often drew His lessons directly from the natural world. Birds, lilies, trees, seeds, and skies—all served as His visual aids to reveal divine truth. Creation itself became His classroom, and the creatures within it His assistants. He taught His disciples to look upon the world not with idle curiosity but with spiritual perception. Every element of nature reflected the wisdom, care, and sovereignty of Jehovah.

Through His use of nature, Jesus reminded His listeners that the visible world continually testifies to the invisible Creator. The heavens declare God's glory (Psalm 19:1), and every living thing proclaims His providence. Jesus' teaching brought this truth to life by connecting the ordinary beauty of nature with the extraordinary reality of God's Kingdom.

His parables and illustrations drawn from creation were more than poetic; they were profoundly theological. They displayed the harmony between revelation and reality—the Word of God written in Scripture and the world of God written in creation.

Both came from the same Author, and both point to His glory.

For teachers and evangelists, following Jesus' example means learning to see the natural world as He saw it—a living canvas painted with spiritual lessons. When rightly interpreted, creation becomes a testimony of God's wisdom, care, and invitation to faith.

Lessons From Birds, Lilies, and Trees

Among Jesus' most memorable natural illustrations are His references to birds, lilies, and trees. Each served as a parable in miniature, carrying profound moral and spiritual lessons.

In Matthew 6:26–30, Jesus said:

"Look at the birds of the air; they do not sow, nor reap, nor gather into barns, yet your heavenly Father feeds them. Are you not worth much more than they?"

Here, Jesus invited His listeners to observe—not merely to glance at—the natural world. The birds became living parables of divine providence. They neither hoard nor worry, yet their needs are met daily by Jehovah's hand. From their contentment, believers learn to trust in God's faithful care.

He continued, "Observe how the lilies of the field grow; they do not toil nor do they spin, yet I say to you that even Solomon in all his glory did not clothe himself like one of these." The lilies, in their effortless beauty, revealed the Creator's aesthetic generosity. Jesus contrasted their transient splendor with human anxiety, showing that the same God who clothes the flowers with glory will clothe His children with grace.

Trees also served as recurring symbols in Jesus' teaching. "Every good tree bears good fruit, but the bad tree bears bad fruit" (Matthew 7:17). Trees illustrated moral integrity and visible evidence of inward faith. Their fruit symbolized character—the outward manifestation of inward devotion.

Through birds, lilies, and trees, Jesus revealed a world infused with divine meaning. Nature was not silent—it spoke to those who had ears to hear. The same world that sustains physical life continually teaches spiritual truth to those who look upon it with faith.

Teaching God's Care Through Nature

One of the most powerful lessons Jesus taught through nature was God's providential care. He used creation as a visible argument against worry and unbelief. Every living creature, every growing plant, and every changing season testified to Jehovah's constant governance of His world.

When Jesus said, "Your heavenly Father knows that you need all these things" (Matthew 6:32), He grounded that assurance in the evidence of nature. The cycle of rain and growth, the feeding of birds, and the blossoming of flowers all confirmed God's active involvement in creation. Nature became a sermon of divine faithfulness.

This teaching was particularly comforting to those who lived close to the land. Farmers and shepherds understood the unpredictability of weather and harvest. By directing their eyes to the sustaining patterns of creation, Jesus anchored faith in observable reality.

Nature does not operate by chance but by divine order. Every sunrise and season testifies to the consistency of God's care. Thus, Jesus' appeal to nature was not sentimental but rational. If God sustains His creation with precision, believers can trust Him to sustain their lives with wisdom and love.

For teachers today, this principle remains vital. Creation offers an inexhaustible resource for illustrating God's attributes—His power in the storm, His beauty in the flower, His provision in the harvest, and His sovereignty in the stars. Every aspect of creation reveals the same truth: God is present, active, and trustworthy.

Creation as a Reflection of Divine Order

Jesus' frequent references to the natural world revealed more than comfort—they displayed divine order. He saw in creation a moral and spiritual structure that mirrored the Creator's wisdom. The same God who designed the seasons to follow in harmony designed spiritual laws that govern human life.

When Jesus spoke of sowing and reaping (Luke 6:38; Galatians 6:7–9), He applied a natural principle to moral conduct. Just as farmers harvest what they plant, so individuals reap the results of their actions—whether righteousness or sin. Creation thus reflects the moral order embedded in reality.

In Mark 4:26–29, the Parable of the Growing Seed describes how a farmer scatters seed, then waits as it grows "he knows not how." The process of germination is unseen yet certain, reflecting the invisible but inevitable work of God's Word in the heart. Nature's laws became Jesus' analogies for spiritual truth.

Creation also revealed God's sovereignty. Winds, waves, and storms obeyed His command. When Jesus calmed the sea (Mark 4:39), He demonstrated that the Creator's authority extends over every element of nature. The world operates not autonomously but under divine direction.

For the believer, recognizing divine order in creation strengthens faith. The harmony of nature is not an accident but an invitation to trust the wisdom of the One who governs it. The moral and natural laws come from the same Lawgiver, uniting the visible and invisible under His sovereign design.

Responding to Worry With Nature's Witness

In His Sermon on the Mount, Jesus addressed one of humanity's most persistent struggles—anxiety. His response was not psychological technique but theological vision. He directed His followers to nature as a living testimony against worry.

"Do not be anxious for your life," He said (Matthew 6:25). His reasoning was simple yet profound: if God feeds the birds and clothes the lilies, how much more will He care for those made in His image? The natural world preaches a daily sermon of trust.

Anxiety, in essence, is forgetfulness of God's providence. Jesus used nature to restore perspective. The birds sing without fear of tomorrow because they trust their Maker's provision. The lilies bloom without labor because they rest in the Creator's design. To worry is to deny the witness of creation, which continually proclaims God's faithfulness.

By observing nature rightly, believers learn both humility and confidence—humility in recognizing their dependence upon God, and confidence in knowing He provides for all His creation. The same Creator who sustains galaxies also tends to sparrows.

In moments of fear or uncertainty, teachers and preachers should remind God's people to look around—to see the ordered beauty of creation and remember that every blade of grass and bird of the air testifies to divine care. The natural world is the antidote to worry because it constantly points back to the Father's faithful provision.

The Creator's Voice in the World He Made

Jesus saw creation as more than evidence of God's existence; He saw it as the voice of the Creator still speaking. Every feature of the natural world proclaimed truth to those who listened with faith. His parables taught that the world was filled with divine communication for those willing to hear.

When He said, "Consider the lilies," He invited His listeners to meditate on creation's message. The verb "consider" implies thoughtful observation—seeing beyond the surface. The believer's task is not merely to admire nature but to interpret its testimony.

The psalmist declared, "The heavens are telling of the glory of God; and the firmament is declaring the work of His hands" (Psalm 19:1). Jesus embodied this same theology in practice. His teaching revealed that the world is not spiritually silent but filled with revelation. The rustle of leaves, the flight of birds, and the patterns of seasons all testify to divine wisdom.

This recognition calls believers to reverence. To exploit or ignore creation is to silence a voice that continually glorifies its Maker. Properly understood, nature is not a rival to Scripture but a companion witness—one revealing God's power and provision, the other His plan and purpose.

Teachers can help their listeners hear the Creator's voice by drawing attention to these natural testimonies. When believers see the world as Jesus did, they learn that faith is not detached from creation but deepened by it. Every sunrise becomes a reminder of resurrection hope; every seed a picture of spiritual rebirth.

Using Creation in Evangelistic Conversations

Jesus' approach to teaching through creation offers an invaluable model for evangelism. Natural illustrations provide a universal bridge to divine truth. Every person, regardless of education or background, can observe the world around them. Creation becomes common ground—a starting point for discussing the Creator.

Paul later echoed this approach when he wrote, "Since the creation of the world His invisible attributes, His eternal power and divine nature, have been clearly seen, being understood through what has been made" (Romans 1:20). The natural world is

God's first witness, preparing hearts for the second—the written Word.

When speaking to unbelievers, Christians can use creation to open hearts to God's reality. The beauty of a flower, the order of the stars, the instincts of animals—all point to design and purpose. From that foundation, one can naturally transition to the gospel, showing that the same Creator who sustains life also redeems it through Christ.

Jesus exemplified this in His teaching. His parables often began with nature but ended with a call to repentance or faith. For instance, in the Parable of the Fig Tree (Luke 13:6–9), He used a tree's fruitfulness to symbolize spiritual readiness. The natural image became a spiritual challenge.

In modern evangelism, creation remains a powerful doorway to the gospel. By drawing attention to the world around us, we direct attention to the One who made it. Every mountain, river, and sky invites worship; every living thing testifies that life comes from the Living God.

Jesus' use of creation in His teaching demonstrates that divine truth is all-encompassing—it fills both Scripture and nature, heaven and earth. To teach as Jesus taught is to open eyes to the Creator's handiwork and to lead hearts from admiration to adoration, from observation to obedience.

When we learn to see the world as He saw it, every sunrise becomes a sermon, every field a parable, and every creature a reminder of the Father's care. In creation, we hear not only the voice of God's power but the whisper of His love.

Chapter 12: Parables From Historical and Cultural Events

Jesus Christ, the Great Teacher, not only drew upon nature and everyday life but also upon the historical and cultural realities familiar to His audience. He used collective memory, recent events, and national identity to bring eternal truth into direct contact with contemporary experience. His listeners lived within the tensions of Roman occupation, Pharisaic legalism, and Jewish nationalism—and Jesus used these very contexts to reveal God's sovereignty, justice, and redemptive purpose.

By referencing known events and familiar circumstances, Jesus made truth immediate and unavoidable. His teaching engaged the intellect and conscience through history's living lessons. Whether speaking of kings and servants, builders and tenants, or current tragedies, He used the events of His day to reveal timeless principles about sin, repentance, and divine authority.

Through these parables, Jesus demonstrated that history is not random but purposeful. Every rise and fall of nations, every act of justice or tragedy, fits within Jehovah's sovereign design. The same God who governed Israel's history governs all human history. Jesus' teaching transformed history into theology and culture into moral instruction, showing that the past and present both testify to divine truth.

Drawing From the Audience's Collective Memory

Jesus frequently appealed to the collective memory of His audience—the shared experiences, traditions, and historical knowledge that shaped their worldview. The people of Israel had a rich national heritage, steeped in Scripture and covenantal identity. By drawing upon these memories, Jesus connected divine revelation to their lived reality.

In the Parable of the Wicked Tenants (Matthew 21:33–46), He referenced the imagery of a vineyard—an image Israel's Scriptures had long associated with the nation itself (Isaiah 5:1–7). His listeners immediately recognized the allusion. The vineyard represented Israel, the owner Jehovah, and the tenants the religious leaders entrusted with spiritual oversight. By invoking a familiar historical symbol, Jesus exposed Israel's repeated pattern of rejecting God's messengers and ultimately His Son.

Similarly, in Matthew 22:1–14, the Parable of the Wedding Feast drew upon Jewish social customs regarding invitations and honor. The people's collective understanding of hospitality and hierarchy heightened the parable's impact. When the invited guests refused to come, the insult was clear—and the moral unmistakable: rejection of divine invitation results in judgment.

By appealing to collective memory, Jesus ensured that His parables were not abstract lessons detached from reality but deeply personal reflections of Israel's spiritual condition. His teaching forced His hearers to see themselves within their own history, making the Word of God both familiar and convicting.

Using Known Events to Impart Moral Lessons

Jesus also referred to known historical and current events to impart moral and spiritual lessons. He used tragedy, injustice, and social occurrences as springboards for eternal truth. His teaching never sensationalized these events; rather, it transformed them into opportunities for repentance and reflection.

In Luke 13:1–5, Jesus mentioned two well-known incidents: Pilate's massacre of Galileans and the collapse of the tower in Siloam. The people of His day debated whether these tragedies were divine punishment. Jesus rejected such superstition and turned the conversation to the universal need for repentance:

"Do you suppose that these Galileans were greater sinners than all other Galileans because they suffered this fate? I tell you, no, but unless you repent, you will all likewise perish."

In doing so, He exposed the fallacy of linking calamity with specific guilt and instead emphasized the urgency of personal repentance. He took current headlines, as it were, and revealed their eternal relevance.

By referencing known events, Jesus gave context to spiritual truth. His lessons were not theoretical but anchored in the real moral crises of the day. This approach made His teaching unavoidable—it demanded a response. Those who heard Him could not dismiss His message as irrelevant; He spoke directly into their world, using the events they discussed to reveal the God they had ignored.

Highlighting God's Sovereignty in History

Jesus' use of historical and cultural references consistently underscored Jehovah's sovereignty over all human affairs. He revealed that history, far from being random or chaotic, unfolds according to divine purpose. The rise and fall of nations, the success or failure of leaders, and the destinies of individuals all move within the boundaries of God's will.

In Matthew 24, Jesus spoke prophetically of the destruction of Jerusalem—a future event for His hearers but one rooted in Israel's historical pattern of rebellion. He warned that the coming desolation would fulfill what had been "spoken of through Daniel the prophet" (v. 15). In this, He showed that even the judgment of nations falls under divine decree. History was not spiraling out of control; it was fulfilling God's prophetic Word.

Jesus also used the historical accounts of Scripture to reinforce moral lessons. When He referenced Noah's generation or Lot's day (Luke 17:26–32), He did so to illustrate the consistency of divine justice. Just as judgment came upon those who ignored God's warnings in the past, it would come again to those who reject truth in the present.

Through these historical parallels, Jesus revealed that the God of history is the same today as He was yesterday—unchanging, just, and sovereign. The events of the past are not distant stories but mirrors reflecting the principles by which God continues to rule.

For teachers today, this truth remains essential. History, both biblical and modern, must be interpreted through the lens of divine sovereignty. Every epoch, empire, and event ultimately points to the fulfillment of God's purposes in Christ.

Correcting Misunderstood Events Through Truth

Jesus also used historical and cultural events to correct misunderstandings about God's character and justice. The Jewish people of His time often interpreted disasters, political oppression, or social inequality through a distorted lens of divine favoritism or wrath. Jesus restored balance by interpreting events through the truth of Scripture.

In John 9:1–3, when the disciples saw a man blind from birth and asked, "Rabbi, who sinned, this man or his parents, that he was born blind?" Jesus answered, "Neither this man nor his parents sinned, but this happened so that the works of God might be displayed in him." In that single statement, Jesus corrected centuries of cultural misconception—that suffering was always a sign of sin—and revealed God's redemptive purpose even in affliction.

Similarly, when addressing Rome's oppression, Jesus refused to align with the political expectations of His time. The Jews anticipated a Messiah who would overthrow Rome, but Jesus redefined the Kingdom of God as spiritual, not political. His parables about kings, servants, and stewardship corrected false hopes of national dominance and redirected them toward divine submission.

Through these corrections, Jesus revealed that truth, not tradition, must interpret history. The events of life—whether tragic or triumphant—find their meaning only in the light of God's revelation. Teachers who follow His example must confront cultural misconceptions with biblical truth, helping listeners see that divine purpose transcends human explanation.

Jesus' Use of National Identity in Teaching

Jesus skillfully engaged the theme of national identity in His parables, both to honor Israel's covenantal history and to challenge its spiritual pride.

He affirmed Israel's unique role in God's plan but exposed the danger of presuming upon that privilege without repentance.

In the Parable of the Two Sons (Matthew 21:28–32), He contrasted one son who refused but later obeyed with another who agreed but failed to act. His application was unmistakable: the repentant sinners entering the Kingdom ahead of the religious elite mirrored how Gentiles would respond to the gospel ahead of unbelieving Israel.

Similarly, in the Parable of the Great Banquet (Luke 14:15–24), those originally invited (symbolizing Israel) rejected the invitation, while the poor, crippled, and outsiders (symbolizing Gentiles) accepted. Through this story, Jesus both acknowledged Israel's privileged place in salvation history and revealed that God's grace would extend beyond national boundaries.

These teachings were revolutionary. They dismantled the false security of heritage and replaced it with the demand for personal faith and obedience. Jesus demonstrated that divine favor is not inherited through ancestry but received through repentance.

For modern teachers, this principle remains relevant. Cultural or denominational identity must never replace genuine devotion. The gospel transcends every human boundary—national, ethnic, or social. In Christ, God calls all people to humble submission under His universal sovereignty.

Current Event Parables in a Biblical Framework

Jesus' use of historical and contemporary references also provides a model for modern teachers seeking to apply biblical truth in a changing world. He showed how to interpret current events through the lens of Scripture, neither ignoring them nor sensationalizing them.

When asked about tragic or political events, Jesus always redirected the discussion from speculation to personal responsibility. He did not encourage political outrage or curiosity about prophecy for its own sake. Instead, He called His hearers to repentance and faith. His approach demonstrated how to bring divine perspective into contemporary conversation.

Today, teachers must follow the same pattern. Whether addressing wars, natural disasters, or cultural shifts, the goal must be to reveal God's sovereignty, justice, and call to righteousness. Every "current event" can become a modern parable when interpreted biblically. The focus must always remain on spiritual lessons rather than political commentary.

Jesus also demonstrated that truth applied to current circumstances gains urgency. His teaching spoke directly to His generation's moral crises—hypocrisy, greed, pride, and unbelief. Teachers today must likewise confront the spiritual issues of their time with the same courage and compassion, always returning to Scripture as the interpretive foundation.

In every generation, history unfolds under God's hand. The teacher who interprets it through divine truth becomes a prophetic voice—one who not only explains what happens but reveals why it matters in light of eternity.

Jesus' use of historical and cultural events in His parables reminds us that divine truth is never detached from time or culture. God's Word speaks to real people in real situations. History, whether ancient or modern, becomes sacred testimony when viewed through the eyes of faith.

The Great Teacher turned every tragedy into a lesson, every custom into a parable, every national event into a call to repentance. To teach as He taught is to see history as His story—the unfolding revelation of God's justice, mercy, and redemption through His Son.

Chapter 13: Teaching With Compassion and Empathy

Jesus Christ, the Great Teacher, combined perfect truth with perfect tenderness. He never compromised doctrine, yet He always communicated it with compassion. His words pierced hearts, not to crush but to heal. He understood that truth spoken without love becomes harsh, while love without truth becomes hollow. His teaching reflected the divine balance—righteousness joined with mercy, conviction mingled with comfort.

Compassion was not an accessory to His message but the essence of His ministry. Every encounter—whether with sinners, doubters, or disciples—flowed from deep empathy. He saw beyond outward appearances into the struggles of the human heart. His understanding was not based on human psychology but on divine insight into human nature.

Jesus' compassion gave credibility to His teaching. People listened because they knew He cared. He was approachable to the broken, patient with the slow to believe, and merciful toward those caught in sin. His instruction was not cold or distant but relational and redemptive. He embodied the truth that to teach as God teaches, one must love as God loves.

Jesus' Deep Understanding of Human Nature

Jesus' teaching revealed His profound understanding of human nature. He knew the motives behind words, the fears behind actions, and the wounds behind rebellion. As John 2:25 states, "He Himself knew what was in man." His omniscient compassion allowed Him to meet people at the point of their deepest need.

When He spoke with Nicodemus (John 3), Jesus discerned his intellectual sincerity and spiritual confusion. Nicodemus was a teacher of Israel yet lacked understanding of spiritual rebirth. Jesus addressed him with patience, not condemnation. He led him step by step from religious knowledge to spiritual truth. His insight into Nicodemus's heart guided His teaching method—gentle correction grounded in eternal truth.

In contrast, when speaking to the rich young ruler (Mark 10:17–22), Jesus perceived that the man's obstacle was not ignorance but attachment to wealth. The Gospel records, "Jesus felt a love for him." That love did not dilute truth; it deepened it. Jesus told him what he needed to hear, not what he wanted to hear. Compassion guided His firmness.

His understanding of human weakness was not theoretical—it was experiential. Hebrews 4:15 explains that Jesus "was tempted in all things as we are, yet without sin." He knew hunger, exhaustion, loneliness, and sorrow. His empathy was born from identification. The One who made humanity also walked among it, feeling its pain without sharing its sin.

This divine understanding shaped His teaching. He did not address humanity as a detached lawgiver but as a compassionate Shepherd. His truth was tailored to the heart before Him—challenging the proud, healing the broken, and guiding the confused.

Identifying With the Weak and Broken

Jesus consistently identified with the weak, the broken, and the marginalized. His compassion was not selective. He did not reserve His attention for the educated or the elite. He taught the crowds, the children, the sick, and the sinners. Each received from Him not only instruction but dignity.

In Matthew 9:36, we read, "Seeing the crowds, He felt compassion for them, because they were distressed and downcast, like sheep without a shepherd." His heart moved before His mouth spoke. Compassion preceded teaching. He saw not just sinners to correct but souls to rescue.

When He encountered the woman at the well (John 4), Jesus crossed social and moral barriers to reach her. He acknowledged her sin but also her thirst for meaning. His teaching was personal, redemptive, and restorative. By revealing Himself as the Messiah, He transformed her from an outcast into a witness.

Similarly, when He met the woman caught in adultery (John 8:1–11), His compassion disarmed the self-righteous while extending mercy to the guilty. He neither condoned her sin nor condemned her soul. "Neither do I condemn you," He said. "Go. From now on sin no more." In that moment, truth and grace stood side by side.

Jesus' identification with the broken fulfilled Isaiah's prophecy: "A bruised reed He will not break, and a dimly burning wick He will not extinguish" (Isaiah 42:3). His gentleness restored rather than crushed. His teaching reached those whom others dismissed.

For teachers today, His example demands humility and tenderness. Those who teach the Word must see beyond behavior to the heart that needs healing. Instruction divorced from compassion alienates; instruction rooted in love transforms.

Addressing Doubts With Gentleness

Jesus never despised sincere doubt. He distinguished between hardened unbelief and honest uncertainty. Where others saw weakness, He saw opportunity for growth. His teaching toward doubters was patient, not punitive.

When Thomas struggled to believe the resurrection (John 20:24–29), Jesus did not rebuke him harshly. Instead, He appeared personally, inviting Thomas to examine His wounds. His words, “Do not be unbelieving, but believing,” combined correction with compassion. Thomas’s faith was restored through encounter, not humiliation.

Likewise, John the Baptist, once the bold herald of the Messiah, later questioned Jesus’ identity from prison (Matthew 11:2–6). Jesus responded not with disappointment but affirmation. He pointed John to the evidence of His works—the blind seeing, the lame walking, and the poor hearing the gospel. Then He honored John publicly, calling him the greatest among those born of women.

Jesus' response to doubt teaches that faith grows through assurance, not coercion. Doubt is not always defiance; it can be the struggle of faith seeking understanding. The Teacher's role is to guide, not to shame.

In ministry, this means meeting doubters where they are—providing truth with gentleness, reason with grace. Compassionate teaching recognizes that faith is often a journey from confusion to conviction. Just as Jesus guided His followers patiently, teachers must nurture spiritual growth without discouragement or pride.

Teaching With Patience and Love

Patience defined Jesus' teaching ministry. His disciples were slow to understand, quick to argue, and prone to fear, yet He bore with them continually. He corrected their errors with firmness but never despair. His endurance was rooted in love.

In Mark 9:33–37, when the disciples debated who was the greatest, Jesus did not rebuke them with harshness. Instead, He sat down, called a child to Himself, and taught a lesson in humility. His patience turned their ambition into instruction.

When Peter denied Him three times, Jesus restored him not with condemnation but with a question repeated three times: "Do you love Me?" (John 21:15–17). Each repetition reaffirmed grace, transforming Peter's failure into faithfulness.

His patience extended even to those who opposed Him. From the cross, He prayed, "Father, forgive them; for they do not know what they are doing" (Luke 23:34). His love endured beyond betrayal, mockery, and pain.

Patience in teaching is not weakness—it is strength under control. It reflects the heart of the Teacher who waits for transformation rather than demands instant perfection. Teachers who embody Christ's patience communicate not only truth but the character of the One who is Truth.

Avoiding Condescension in Instruction

Jesus never condescended in His teaching, though He was infinitely greater than His hearers. His authority was divine, yet His tone was humble. He spoke as one who served, not as one who dominated.

In Matthew 11:29, He invited, "Take My yoke upon you, and learn from Me, for I am gentle and humble in heart." His authority attracted rather than intimidated. He did not use His knowledge to elevate Himself but to elevate others toward understanding.

Condescension destroys communication. It alienates learners and hardens hearts. Jesus, by contrast, built bridges through humility. He washed His disciples' feet, modeling the principle that true teachers must first be servants. Instruction without humility becomes self-promotion; teaching with humility becomes transformation.

Even when addressing the ignorant or the erring, Jesus maintained dignity without disdain. To the Samaritan woman, He spoke truth without ridicule. To Zacchaeus, the despised tax collector, He extended fellowship without reproach. His kindness opened the way for repentance.

Christian teachers must imitate this spirit. Authority in teaching does not justify arrogance. Knowledge must serve, not lord over others. The teacher's role is not to impress but to enlighten, not to command admiration but to inspire obedience to Christ.

The Role of Emotional Intelligence in Evangelism

Jesus demonstrated perfect emotional intelligence—the ability to understand and respond to the emotions of others with wisdom and grace. He was fully attuned to the feelings, fears, and hopes of those He taught. His communication was both truthful and tender because He understood the emotional landscape of the human heart.

He wept with the grieving (John 11:35), rejoiced with the repentant (Luke 15:7), and felt compassion for the hungry (Mark 8:2). His emotions were never self-centered but always others-focused. They informed His teaching rather than clouded it.

When confronted with hostility, He responded with calm authority. When approached by the desperate, He offered gentle assurance. He balanced firmness with empathy, rebuke with mercy. His mastery of emotion made His teaching not only intellectually sound but emotionally resonant.

Evangelism requires this same spiritual discernment. The gospel addresses both mind and heart. Teachers must understand their audience's fears, doubts, and struggles. Empathy opens the door for truth to enter. A message spoken without sensitivity may be right in content but wrong in impact.

Jesus' emotional intelligence reflected divine wisdom. He knew when to speak and when to remain silent, when to comfort and when to confront.

Teachers who learn from His example will communicate the gospel effectively—combining conviction with compassion, clarity with care.

Jesus' compassion and empathy were not sentimental traits but expressions of divine perfection. They gave power to His teaching, warmth to His truth, and hope to His hearers. He was both the Shepherd who knew His sheep and the Teacher who knew their hearts.

To teach as Jesus taught is to love as He loved—to combine unwavering truth with unyielding tenderness. Compassion gives credibility to truth, and empathy gives voice to grace. In the hands of such a teacher, the Word of God does not merely inform; it transforms.

Chapter 14: Imitating Jesus' Simplicity in Our Teaching

Jesus Christ, the Great Teacher, demonstrated that divine truth, though infinite in depth, can be expressed with absolute simplicity. He never obscured His message behind complex terminology or philosophical abstraction. Instead, He made profound truths understandable to fishermen, farmers, and children. The One who "spoke as no man ever spoke" (John 7:46) revealed that true wisdom is not shown in the ability to confuse but in the power to clarify.

Simplicity was not a reduction of truth but a refinement of expression. Jesus distilled eternal realities into vivid images, short sayings, and memorable parables. His teaching was neither shallow nor simplistic—it was accessible without losing accuracy, profound without becoming complicated. He taught that God's message must be communicated in a way that penetrates both the intellect and the heart.

For those who would teach and evangelize today, imitating Jesus' simplicity is not optional—it is essential. Complexity often reflects human pride, while clarity reflects divine wisdom. To reach both the learned and the humble, teachers must learn to present truth in the language of life, as Jesus did.

Breaking Down Doctrinal Complexity

Jesus faced the same challenge that every teacher faces: conveying eternal truths to finite minds. Yet He never allowed doctrinal depth to become doctrinal difficulty. He broke down complex theological realities into concrete terms that ordinary people could grasp.

When teaching about the new birth, He spoke of being "born again" (John 3:3–7). When revealing faith's power, He compared it to a mustard seed (Matthew 17:20). When describing His atoning work, He likened Himself to a shepherd laying down His life for the sheep (John 10:11). These simple metaphors communicated unfathomable truth in relatable form.

Jesus' approach was not to dilute doctrine but to distill it. He simplified without compromising accuracy. His illustrations clarified divine mysteries without diminishing their majesty. The incarnation, redemption, and Kingdom of God—all were explained through images familiar to the common listener.

This example teaches that effective communication of truth is not achieved by multiplying words or complexity, but by mastering clarity. Every teacher must ask: *Am I making truth more understandable or more obscure?* The goal of teaching is not to impress the mind but to illuminate it, so that God's truth may penetrate the heart.

Paul followed this same principle when he wrote, "We have renounced the things hidden because of shame, not walking in craftiness... but by the manifestation of truth commending ourselves to every man's conscience" (2 Corinthians 4:2). The goal of all doctrinal instruction must be accessibility, not academic obscurity.

Teachers must therefore strive, as Jesus did, to make the Word of God clear to every listener—whether simple or scholarly—because truth concealed by complexity fails its purpose.

Teaching Young and Old Alike

One of the most remarkable features of Jesus' teaching was its universal accessibility. His words could reach both the uneducated and the educated, the young and the aged, the poor and the rich. His simplicity ensured that no one was excluded from understanding.

Children were drawn to Him instinctively. In Matthew 19:14, He said, "Allow the children to come to Me, and do not forbid them; for the kingdom of heaven belongs to such as these." His teaching resonated with their innocence and curiosity. When He used simple stories—a lost coin, a shepherd seeking a sheep—children could comprehend the message even as adults found deeper meaning within it.

At the same time, scholars like Nicodemus and rulers like the centurion recognized the authority and depth of His words. His simplicity carried intellectual credibility. The same truth that fed the lambs nourished the mature sheep.

True teaching, therefore, is both inclusive and scalable. It must reach across ages and levels of understanding. This does not mean oversimplifying to the point of shallowness but presenting truth with clarity and adaptability. The Word of God contains nourishment for every spiritual stage, and the teacher's task is to serve it in digestible portions.

In the Church, sermons and studies often err in two directions—either oversimplifying truth to appease the indifferent or overcomplicating it to impress the informed. Jesus avoided both extremes. His teaching was layered: the surface was clear enough for a child, yet the depth was endless for the seeker. Every Christian teacher must learn to emulate this divine inclusiveness—reaching young and old alike with the same life-giving Word.

Avoiding Religious Jargon

One of the barriers that often obstructs effective teaching and evangelism is the overuse of religious jargon—words and expressions familiar to insiders but foreign to outsiders. Jesus avoided this completely. His language was drawn from life, not from theological vocabulary.

He did not speak in terms of "soteriology," "eschatology," or "sanctification." Instead, He spoke of being "born again," of a "harvest," of a "kingdom," of "living water," and of a "house built on rock." His words painted pictures, not abstractions. The simplest listener could grasp His meaning, yet the most thoughtful could ponder it endlessly.

Religious jargon often arises from a sincere desire to be precise, but it frequently obscures rather than clarifies. It can make the teacher appear knowledgeable while leaving the listener uninstructed. Jesus, however, chose clarity over complexity and life over lecture.

For example, when teaching about repentance, He said, "Unless you repent, you will all likewise perish" (Luke 13:3). He did not explain repentance with academic definition but illustrated it through the story of the Prodigal Son—turning from sin and returning to the Father.

When speaking of justification and grace, He did not use technical terms; He told of a Pharisee and a tax collector praying in the temple, the humble one going home justified (Luke 18:9–14). These vivid examples captured divine truths more effectively than abstract terminology ever could.

Teachers who imitate Jesus' example will use plain, powerful language rooted in Scripture and daily life. Words should serve as windows, not walls—transparent instruments that reveal truth rather than conceal it. Simplicity in speech magnifies the authority of Scripture because it reflects the nature of divine revelation itself—clear, truthful, and accessible.

Using Memorable Illustrations

Jesus filled His teaching with vivid, memorable illustrations that captured both attention and understanding. His analogies were drawn from life's ordinary realities—light, salt, bread, water, seeds, and shepherds. Each image engraved truth upon the memory.

In the Sermon on the Mount, He declared, "You are the salt of the earth... You are the light of the world" (Matthew 5:13–14). These metaphors were simple enough for any listener to remember yet profound enough to guide a lifetime of discipleship.

In John 15, He described Himself as the "true vine" and His followers as "branches." The agricultural image illustrated the dependence of believers upon Him for spiritual life. In one picture, He communicated the essence of Christian sanctification and fruit-bearing.

His illustrations were not merely decorative but functional. They turned abstract truth into visible form. They engaged the imagination, awakened conscience, and made doctrine personal.

Teachers must recover this skill. Illustration is not entertainment—it is illumination. It anchors truth in the mind through imagery that appeals to the senses. Jesus' use of illustration demonstrates that memorable teaching is not about eloquence but about connection. A teacher who can translate divine principles into relatable images will reach both heart and mind.

Moreover, illustrations drawn from Scripture itself carry divine authority. Jesus did not rely on speculation or creativity detached from truth. His imagery revealed and reinforced biblical reality. Teachers who imitate Him will speak vividly but biblically, using stories and symbols that magnify the message rather than the messenger.

Presenting Christ Clearly to the Lost

Jesus' simplicity in teaching found its highest expression in presenting Himself clearly as the way of salvation. He did not hide behind parables when revealing the core of the gospel: "I am the way, and the truth, and the life; no one comes to the Father but through Me" (John 14:6).

His message was direct and unmistakable. He called sinners to repentance, not philosophy; to faith, not speculation. His appeal was not to intellectual pride but to spiritual need. When speaking to the Samaritan woman, He revealed Himself plainly: "I who speak to you am He" (John 4:26). Salvation was not a concept to analyze but a Person to trust.

In evangelism, clarity is the greatest act of compassion. To obscure the gospel behind human eloquence or theological jargon is to withhold life from those who need it most. The sinner's heart must hear the simple, unadorned truth: that Christ died for our sins, was raised from the dead, and offers forgiveness and eternal life to all who believe.

Paul expressed this same commitment: "When I came to you, brethren, I did not come with superiority of speech or of wisdom, proclaiming to you the testimony of God. For I determined to know nothing among you except Jesus Christ, and Him crucified" (1 Corinthians 2:1–2).

The modern teacher and evangelist must echo that resolve. The aim is not to impress minds but to save souls. Presenting Christ clearly, as Jesus did, ensures that the focus remains on the Savior, not the speaker.

The Simplicity of the Gospel Message

At the heart of Jesus' teaching lies the greatest simplicity of all—the gospel message itself. Though theologians may write volumes to explain it, its essence can be stated in one sentence: "For God so loved the world that He gave His only begotten Son, that whoever believes in Him shall not perish, but have eternal life" (John 3:16).

This is divine simplicity. The greatest truth in the universe is comprehensible to a child. Salvation does not depend on intellectual mastery but on humble faith. The gospel is not a code to decipher but a call to believe.

Jesus never burdened His hearers with complex systems of theology. He invited them to trust, follow, and obey. His message was personal, direct, and transformational. The simplicity of the gospel does not mean it lacks depth—it means it is universally accessible. Every person, regardless of education or background, can understand the way to salvation through Christ.

Teachers must guard this simplicity. When the gospel is entangled in human speculation or philosophical elaboration, its power is diminished. The message of the cross must remain clear, compelling, and uncomplicated: humanity's sin, God's love, Christ's sacrifice, and the promise of forgiveness through faith.

In every generation, the task of the Church is not to modernize the gospel but to make it clear. To imitate Jesus' simplicity is to trust that God's truth, plainly spoken, still changes hearts.

Jesus' simplicity was divine wisdom clothed in human words. His teaching reached shepherds and scholars alike because He spoke the language of truth untainted by pride. He modeled the kind of clarity every teacher should seek—truth without distortion, depth without confusion, and conviction without complication.

To teach as Jesus taught is to love the listener enough to make truth understandable. It is to present the gospel so simply that even a child can believe it and yet so profoundly that the wisest mind will never exhaust it.

Chapter 15: Imitating Jesus' Use of Questions in Evangelism

Jesus Christ, the Great Teacher, used questions not merely to gather information but to reveal truth, expose error, and lead His hearers toward repentance and faith. His questions were purposeful, probing, and precise. They invited reflection, demanded honesty, and revealed the heart's true condition. Unlike the rabbis or philosophers of His time, Jesus did not engage in speculative debate. His questions were divine instruments of conviction and illumination.

From His youth to His final days, Jesus' use of questioning displayed unparalleled wisdom. Even at the age of twelve, when found in the temple among the teachers of the Law, He was "sitting among the teachers, both listening to them and asking them questions" (Luke 2:46). The Greek word used there for "asking" (*eperōtaō*) is not the common term for a child's curiosity; it is a forensic term used in legal contexts—referring to a formal line of questioning, such as that conducted in a judicial proceeding. Jesus was not passively learning; He was engaging them as one who tested and examined. His questions had the authority of one presenting divine truth before human judges.

Throughout His ministry, Jesus continued to employ this method. He questioned His opponents not to humiliate them but to expose hypocrisy, to clarify truth, and to lead the humble toward salvation. His use of questions remains one of the most powerful evangelistic and teaching methods available to the Church. Every Christian who seeks to teach or share the gospel can learn from His divine example of using questions as a means of revelation and persuasion.

Preparing Questions to Challenge Assumptions

Jesus' questions were never spontaneous or careless. Each was carefully crafted to challenge false assumptions and to turn the hearer's mind toward divine truth. He used questions as precision tools—piercing through layers of self-deception, tradition, and pride.

In Matthew 22:41–46, Jesus asked the Pharisees, "What do you think about the Christ, whose son is He?" When they answered, "The son of David," He followed with another question: "Then how does David in the Spirit call Him 'Lord,' saying, 'The Lord said to my Lord, "Sit at My right hand, until I put Your enemies beneath Your feet"?'" The question cornered them with Scripture itself. They could neither deny the verse nor reconcile it with their limited view of the Messiah. The text says, "No one was able to answer Him a word."

This demonstrates that Jesus' questions were more than conversational—they were revelatory. He prepared them with divine precision to dismantle false beliefs. His method teaches that effective evangelism requires both spiritual discernment and preparation. Teachers and evangelists must think through the assumptions their audience holds and frame questions that reveal those assumptions for what they are.

The believer who studies the Word deeply, prays for wisdom, and learns from Jesus' model can ask questions that penetrate the heart rather than merely entertain the mind. Preparation transforms a question from idle curiosity into a tool of conviction.

Asking to Reveal Heart Conditions

Jesus' questions often went beneath the surface of intellect to uncover the state of the heart. His goal was not to win arguments but to awaken conscience.

He questioned people in ways that revealed what they loved, feared, and trusted most.

When the rich young ruler approached Him, asking, "What must I do to inherit eternal life?" (Mark 10:17), Jesus responded with a series of questions designed to expose his heart. After affirming the commandments, Jesus asked, "Why do you call Me good? No one is good except God alone." This question forced the man to consider whether he truly recognized Jesus' divine identity or merely viewed Him as a moral teacher. Later, by instructing him to sell all and follow Him, Jesus uncovered his misplaced trust in wealth.

Similarly, in Luke 10:25–37, when a lawyer asked, "Who is my neighbor?" Jesus did not answer directly but told the Parable of the Good Samaritan. At the end, He asked, "Which of these three do you think proved to be a neighbor?" The question forced the listener to confront his own prejudice and hypocrisy. Jesus' questioning led him to self-conviction rather than external correction.

The purpose of such questions is not to shame but to reveal. People resist being told they are wrong, but they cannot escape the realization when truth emerges from their own conscience. Jesus' approach teaches evangelists to use questions that lead individuals to see themselves as God sees them—to diagnose before prescribing, to reveal before instructing.

Drawing Out Repentance Through Dialogue

Jesus used dialogue to draw sinners gently toward repentance. He engaged them in conversation that required self-examination and moral decision. His questions became spiritual mirrors reflecting the heart's true image.

When He met the Samaritan woman at the well (John 4:7–26), His conversation began with a simple request: "Give Me a drink." From there, He asked questions and made statements that revealed her spiritual thirst. "Where is your husband?" was not asked for information—He already knew the answer—but to awaken her awareness of sin and need. His gentle questioning led her from evasion to confession, and ultimately to recognition of Him as the Messiah.

Likewise, after Peter denied Him three times, the resurrected Jesus restored him through a series of three questions: "Do you love Me?" (John 21:15–17). Each repetition corresponded to a denial, offering forgiveness through reflection. The questions were neither accusatory nor rhetorical; they invited repentance through love.

This divine method demonstrates that repentance cannot be coerced; it must be drawn out. Jesus' questions led people to discover their guilt in the light of His grace. They allowed the sinner to voice his own need, making repentance genuine and heartfelt.

Christian teachers and evangelists must learn to use dialogue in the same way—to speak truth that provokes self-awareness, not self-defense. The right question, guided by the Spirit and grounded in Scripture, can do more to awaken repentance than a hundred statements of accusation.

Questions That Expose False Teachings

Jesus' questions often served to expose the falseness of human traditions and theological errors. Rather than directly denouncing His opponents, He led them to contradict themselves through their own words. His questions were both disarming and devastating, revealing the bankruptcy of their reasoning.

In Matthew 21:23–27, the chief priests and elders challenged His authority: "By what authority are You doing these things?" Jesus replied, "I also will ask you one thing, which if you tell Me, I will also tell you by what authority I do these things: The baptism of John—was it from heaven or from men?" They reasoned among themselves and could not answer without condemning themselves. His question exposed their hypocrisy—they cared more about public approval than divine truth.

Another example appears in Mark 3:4, where Jesus asked, "Is it lawful to do good or to do harm on the Sabbath, to save a life or to kill?" His question silenced the Pharisees, revealing the cruelty of their rigid legalism. What they refused to admit, His question made undeniable—that their traditions had obscured the law's true purpose.

Jesus' questioning technique revealed that false teaching collapses under honest examination. It needs only the light of truth to expose its darkness. Teachers today can follow this same model by using Scripture-based questions that confront error indirectly, compelling people to recognize inconsistencies between their beliefs and God's Word.

The goal, however, must always be restoration, not humiliation. Jesus used truth to rescue, not to ridicule. The teacher's task is to uncover falsehood graciously, leading others toward repentance and sound doctrine.

Using Questions to Promote Action

Jesus never asked questions for the sake of intellectual debate. His inquiries demanded response and action. He called His listeners to make choices—to obey, to repent, to believe, to follow. His questions transformed passive listeners into active participants in the truth.

When He asked, "Why do you call Me, 'Lord, Lord,' and do not do what I say?" (Luke 6:46), He confronted the disconnect between verbal confession and actual obedience. The question forced self-examination: if He is truly Lord, then His authority must produce submission.

When a paralytic man lay before Him, Jesus asked, "Do you wish to get well?" (John 5:6). At first glance, the question seems unnecessary. Yet it probed the man's will, not his condition. Healing required faith and desire; Jesus' question stirred both.

Even in evangelism, Jesus' questions often led to decisive moments. "Who do you say that I am?" (Matthew 16:15) pressed the disciples to personal conviction. Peter's answer—"You are the Christ, the Son of the living God"—marked a defining act of faith.

Questions that promote action do not allow the hearer to remain neutral. They move truth from theory to application. Evangelistic conversations should therefore aim not merely to inform but to invite response. The teacher must speak as Jesus did—with questions that call for decision, pressing the soul toward obedience and transformation.

Guiding Toward Personal Reflection

Jesus' questions also guided His hearers into deep personal reflection. He did not force truth upon them but led them to discover it. His questions acted as spiritual signposts, directing their thoughts toward self-examination and revelation.

When He asked, "For what will it profit a man if he gains the whole world and forfeits his soul?" (Mark 8:36), He confronted humanity's misplaced priorities. The question echoed in the conscience long after He had spoken. Its power lay not in its complexity but in its penetrating simplicity—it demanded that each listener weigh temporal gain against eternal loss.

In Luke 6:41–42, He asked, "Why do you look at the speck that is in your brother's eye, but do not notice the log that is in your own eye?" The image was humorous yet convicting. It exposed hypocrisy while inviting introspection. The question forced self-awareness and personal accountability.

Jesus' method teaches that effective evangelism and teaching must not merely tell people what to think but lead them to think. Reflection deepens conviction. Truth discovered personally is truth retained permanently.

When believers guide others through questions that provoke thought, conscience, and humility, they follow the same path the Master walked. His questions were more than speech—they were instruments of divine revelation, shaping the heart to receive the Word.

From His first appearance in the temple at twelve years old, where He questioned the teachers of the Law with legal precision, to His final dialogues with disciples and opponents alike, Jesus demonstrated the divine art of questioning. His inquiries revealed truth, exposed hypocrisy, drew out repentance, and guided hearts toward faith and obedience.

To imitate Jesus' use of questions in evangelism is to learn the holy skill of listening deeply, thinking wisely, and speaking strategically. The teacher or evangelist who asks as Jesus asked will not merely win debates but win souls—leading others to see themselves, their sin, and their Savior in the mirror of divine truth.

Chapter 16: Imitating Jesus' Logical Approach to Teaching

Jesus Christ, the Great Teacher, was the perfect embodiment of reason united with revelation. His teaching was never irrational or mystical. He appealed to both the heart and the mind, combining moral authority with flawless logic. As the Word made flesh (John 1:14), He not only spoke truth but reasoned it. His arguments were never based on emotion, manipulation, or intimidation, but on the firm foundation of Scripture and divine logic.

Throughout His ministry, Jesus displayed a profound ability to expose error, dismantle false reasoning, and build sound arguments that could not be refuted. His logic was not human philosophy but the wisdom of God applied through reasoned communication. In every encounter—whether with Pharisees, Sadducees, or disciples—He demonstrated that truth stands secure under the brightest light of examination.

To imitate Jesus' logical approach to teaching is to restore the unity between faith and reason. It is to recognize that the God who commands us to love Him with all our heart and soul also commands us to love Him "with all [our] mind" (Matthew 22:37). Teachers and evangelists who follow His example will train believers to think biblically, reason carefully, and communicate truth persuasively—always with humility and reverence.

Correcting Error Without Arrogance

Jesus' correction of error was marked by both firmness and gentleness. He confronted falsehood directly but without arrogance or hostility. His goal was always restoration, not humiliation.

When the Sadducees denied the resurrection, He answered them decisively but graciously: "You are mistaken, not understanding the Scriptures nor the power of God" (Matthew 22:29). His words were not sarcastic or condescending; they were diagnostic. He identified the precise cause of their error—ignorance of Scripture and unbelief in God's power. His logic then corrected both by citing Exodus 3:6, showing that Jehovah is "the God of Abraham, the God of Isaac, and the God of Jacob," therefore "not the God of the dead but of the living." His reasoning was precise, textual, and irrefutable.

This example reveals how to correct error effectively. It begins with identifying the root—whether misunderstanding, misinterpretation, or misapplication of Scripture—and addressing it with clarity and grace. Jesus never allowed falsehood to go unchallenged, yet He never resorted to pride or insult. His authority was moral as well as intellectual.

Teachers must follow His balance. Arrogance undermines truth; humility amplifies it. The correction of error should arise from love for both truth and people. A teacher who corrects with gentleness preserves credibility and opens hearts to transformation.

Paul later reflected this same principle when instructing Timothy: "The Lord's bond-servant must not be quarrelsome, but be kind to all, able to teach, patient when wronged, with gentleness correcting those who are in opposition" (2 Timothy 2:24–25). Jesus' logic was persuasive because it was clothed in compassion.

Distinguishing Sound Doctrine From Tradition

One of Jesus' most consistent applications of logical reasoning was His exposure of the difference between divine doctrine and human tradition. The religious leaders of His time had built elaborate systems of man-made rules that obscured the true intent of God's law. Jesus' logic cut through this confusion, separating divine authority from human invention.

In Mark 7:6–13, He confronted the Pharisees for elevating their traditions above Scripture. They criticized His disciples for eating with unwashed hands, claiming it violated purity laws. Jesus responded logically and scripturally: "Neglecting the commandment of God, you hold to the tradition of men." He then cited the command to honor one's father and mother, exposing how their tradition of *Corban* (dedicating possessions to the temple) contradicted God's Word.

His reasoning was airtight: if a human tradition nullifies God's command, it is invalid. Jesus showed that true doctrine must always align with Scripture, not human authority. He appealed not to emotion but to logic rooted in revelation.

Teachers today must likewise distinguish between what is biblically commanded and what is merely culturally inherited. Many modern errors arise from confusing tradition with truth. By following Jesus' logical example, teachers can expose false assumptions and restore the authority of God's Word as the final standard.

Sound doctrine is consistent, coherent, and scripturally grounded. Tradition, when elevated above truth, becomes idolatry of the mind. Logic grounded in Scripture protects the Church from such drift.

Developing Reasoning Skills in Others

Jesus did not simply demonstrate logic—He developed it in His followers. His teaching method trained the mind as well as the heart. He asked questions, challenged conclusions, and encouraged discernment. He wanted His disciples to *think* as well as to *believe*.

In Matthew 16:8–11, when His disciples misunderstood His warning about the "leaven of the Pharisees," He used reasoning to guide them: "Do you not yet understand or remember the five loaves of the five thousand...?" His argument appealed to memory, observation, and deduction. He led them step by step from confusion to clarity.

Likewise, in Luke 24:25–27, on the road to Emmaus, Jesus reasoned with two disheartened disciples, saying, "Was it not necessary for the Christ to suffer these things and to enter into His glory?" Then, "beginning with Moses and with all the prophets, He explained to them the things concerning Himself in all the Scriptures." His reasoning was cumulative and evidential, moving from prophecy to fulfillment.

Jesus' goal was not passive acceptance but active understanding. He modeled how to analyze evidence, interpret Scripture, and connect truth coherently. His teaching made thinkers of His disciples, not merely followers.

For teachers today, this provides an essential model. Rather than spoon-feeding conclusions, we must equip learners to reason biblically. This involves asking guiding questions, encouraging examination of Scripture, and training believers to test every claim by the Word of God. Logic strengthens faith when it is exercised under submission to divine revelation.

Sound teaching produces reasoning disciples—Christians who can discern truth from error, who think scripturally rather than sentimentally. This is how the Church grows in both knowledge and stability.

Jesus' Arguments and Their Scriptural Basis

Every argument Jesus made rested firmly upon Scripture. He never appealed to popular opinion, tradition, or emotion as the final authority. His reasoning was always textual, contextual, and theological.

When tempted by Satan in the wilderness (Matthew 4:1–11), Jesus responded to each temptation with, "It is written." His logic followed a simple but unassailable structure: divine command supersedes human desire. Satan's deceitful reasoning was demolished by the authority and clarity of Scripture.

When confronted about divorce (Matthew 19:3–9), Jesus again reasoned from Scripture: "Have you not read that He who created them from the beginning made them male and female?" He cited Genesis 1 and 2, establishing the permanence of marriage as divine design. His argument was deductive: if God joined them together in creation, man has no authority to separate them.

Jesus also used analogical reasoning grounded in Scripture. In Matthew 12:3–7, He defended His disciples' actions on the Sabbath by citing David's eating of the consecrated bread and the priests' temple work. His argument followed the principle of *kal va-chomer* (Hebrew "light and heavy")—if exceptions exist under lesser conditions, how much more under greater divine purpose.

Jesus' logic was therefore inseparable from revelation. He demonstrated that Scripture interprets Scripture and that divine truth always aligns with sound reasoning. The teacher who wishes to reason like Jesus must know Scripture deeply and apply it accurately, letting the Word itself form the argument's foundation.

A Model for Debate and Apologetics

Jesus' logical method offers the perfect model for biblical debate and apologetics. His engagements with opponents were firm, fair, and focused on truth rather than personal victory. He exposed falsehood through calm reasoning and Scriptural clarity.

When challenged about paying taxes to Caesar (Matthew 22:15–22), Jesus saw through the trap. His answer, "Render to Caesar the things that are Caesar's, and to God the things that are God's," demonstrated flawless logic. He affirmed civil responsibility without compromising divine authority. His reasoning balanced principles that others saw as opposites.

In John 8, when religious leaders brought Him the woman caught in adultery, they sought to trap Him between mercy and law. Jesus' response—"He who is without sin among you, let him be the first to throw a stone"—was both moral and logical. His reasoning revealed that their application of the Law was hypocritical, for they were guilty of sin themselves.

These examples show that Jesus' approach to conflict was reasoned, not reactionary. He never resorted to emotional manipulation or rhetoric. His debates were rooted in principle, His conclusions irrefutable.

Christian apologetics must mirror this pattern. Defending the faith is not about intellectual triumph but about unveiling truth. Teachers must cultivate clarity, composure, and scriptural reasoning. The goal is not to defeat an opponent but to glorify God by demonstrating that His Word stands against every false argument (2 Corinthians 10:5).

The apologist who reasons with Jesus' balance—truth with grace, logic with love—becomes both a defender and a witness.

Teaching That Trains the Mind and Heart

Jesus' logical teaching was never cold or abstract. He united reason and revelation, ensuring that truth reached not only the intellect but also the conscience. His goal was transformation through understanding.

When He taught the Great Commandment—"Love the Lord your God with all your heart, and with all your soul, and with all your mind" (Matthew 22:37)—He affirmed that thinking rightly is part of loving rightly. The mind renewed by truth serves the heart renewed by grace.

Jesus trained His disciples to think logically so that they might love wisely. His parables often ended with statements such as "He who has ears to hear, let him hear," inviting meditation and comprehension. Understanding was not an end but a means to obedience.

Sound reasoning produces sound living. A mind anchored in truth resists deception; a heart guided by reasoned faith endures temptation. Jesus' teaching therefore cultivated balanced disciples—those whose faith was both intelligent and heartfelt.

Teachers today must follow this pattern. Emotional appeal alone produces shallow commitment; intellectualism alone produces sterile faith. True Christian instruction trains both mind and heart to function in harmony under the authority of Scripture.

The teacher who reasons as Jesus reasoned will help learners not only to understand what is true but to love why it is true—and to live accordingly.

Jesus' logical approach to teaching reveals that faith and reason are not adversaries but allies. His example calls every teacher to combine conviction with clarity, courage with humility, and intellect with compassion.

To imitate Jesus is to speak with precision, think with Scripture, and reason with grace. His logic was divine light applied to human darkness—truth that not only informs but transforms. In every generation, the Church needs teachers who, like the Master, can reason from the Scriptures, refute error with humility, and train minds that love God's Word with all their strength.

Chapter 17: Imitating Jesus' Use of Illustrations and Stories

Jesus Christ, the Great Teacher, was the supreme communicator of divine truth. His words penetrated hearts not because of mere eloquence but because He illustrated eternal realities through stories, analogies, and images drawn from daily life. He turned fields, lamps, coins, vines, and sheep into lessons of faith and obedience. His illustrations were not decorative additions to His teaching—they were essential vehicles of revelation. Through them, He made the invisible visible, the abstract concrete, and the eternal unforgettable.

Jesus' use of stories revealed divine wisdom in the art of communication. He understood that the human mind grasps truth most effectively when it can see, not merely hear, when it can visualize truth rather than simply define it. His illustrations created mental pictures that remained long after the sound of His voice had faded.

For those who teach, preach, or evangelize, Jesus' model provides a divine blueprint for clarity and connection. His teaching methods remind us that truth must be both accurate and accessible, powerful yet personal, doctrinal yet relatable. When we imitate His use of illustrations and stories, we follow the pattern of the Master who taught hearts as well as minds.

Crafting Biblical Illustrations for Today

Jesus' illustrations were always rooted in biblical truth, never in speculation or fiction for entertainment's sake. Every parable, metaphor, or analogy He used served one purpose—to reveal spiritual reality through the framework of daily experience. Teachers who follow His example must ensure that their illustrations are theologically sound and serve Scripture rather than overshadow it.

In the Parable of the Sower (Matthew 13:3–9), Jesus described four types of soil to illustrate four responses to the Word of God. His story was simple, yet its spiritual depth continues to instruct believers across generations. The imagery of seed and soil transformed abstract doctrines—reception, faith, and perseverance—into living pictures.

Likewise, the Parable of the Lost Sheep (Luke 15:3–7) presented divine compassion in tangible form. The shepherd's search for the one straying sheep revealed God's relentless mercy toward sinners. The story carried the heart of the gospel in a single, unforgettable image.

Modern teachers can follow this same principle. When crafting illustrations, they must remain faithful to the biblical message. Every example, story, or metaphor should point back to Scripture, reinforcing its truth rather than replacing it. The purpose of illustration is illumination, not distraction.

Illustrations that flow from biblical principles and daily reality carry divine weight. Whether drawn from nature, history, personal testimony, or contemporary life, they must always lead listeners to the same destination—the truth of God's Word.

Teaching with Clarity Through Analogy

Jesus' analogies transformed complex ideas into clear, memorable expressions. His use of analogy bridged the gap between the seen and the unseen, making heavenly truth understandable to earthly minds.

When explaining the Kingdom of Heaven, He compared it to a mustard seed that grows into a great tree (Matthew 13:31–32), to leaven that spreads through dough (Matthew 13:33), and to treasure hidden in a field (Matthew 13:44). Each analogy revealed a facet of divine truth—growth, influence, and value. By using familiar imagery, Jesus communicated profound theology without losing simplicity.

In John 15:5, He declared, "I am the vine, you are the branches." The analogy illustrated the believer's dependence upon Him for life and fruitfulness. This one statement conveys the entire doctrine of sanctification more powerfully than pages of abstract explanation.

Analogy is the bridge between comprehension and conviction. It connects what people already know to what they must yet understand. Jesus' analogies were never vague comparisons; they were precise and purposeful. They carried truth from the mind to the conscience.

Teachers who imitate Jesus must therefore study the art of analogy. When explaining Scripture, they should use comparisons that clarify rather than confuse, that reveal rather than obscure. Analogies must never replace doctrine but illuminate it, as light illuminates a jewel's facets without altering its nature.

Through careful, prayerful analogy, truth becomes not only understood but unforgettable.

Making the Invisible Visible

Jesus specialized in revealing unseen realities through visible imagery. His teaching consistently drew attention from the physical to the spiritual, from the temporal to the eternal. Every visible object became a window through which His listeners could glimpse the Kingdom of God.

He used light to describe truth and righteousness: "You are the light of the world" (Matthew 5:14). He used salt to depict moral influence and preservation: "You are the salt of the earth" (Matthew 5:13). He used water to represent the Holy Spirit's life-giving power: "Whoever drinks of the water that I will give him shall never thirst" (John 4:14).

Through such imagery, Jesus trained His listeners to perceive spiritual significance in the ordinary. The created world became a living classroom of divine revelation. His teaching fulfilled Psalm 19:1—"The heavens are telling of the glory of God." Every element of creation became a sermon when interpreted through His words.

This method remains vital for teachers today. Making the invisible visible means connecting divine truth to tangible experience. For example, a teacher might illustrate faith through the act of planting a seed—trusting the unseen growth beneath the soil. Or one might demonstrate forgiveness through the image of a debt erased.

When we follow Jesus' model, we turn abstract theology into experiential truth. Learners begin to *see* what they believe, and belief deepens into conviction. Jesus' method teaches that divine truth is never distant; it is woven into the very fabric of life, waiting to be revealed through Spirit-guided illustration.

Using Common Life Events to Teach Doctrine

Jesus often used ordinary events—weddings, feasts, harvests, fishing trips, and family disputes—to teach eternal truths. His teaching sanctified the common by revealing the divine within it. He transformed everyday experiences into lessons on salvation, judgment, mercy, and discipleship.

The Parable of the Wedding Feast (Matthew 22:1–14) used a familiar social event to portray the invitation of God's Kingdom. The Parable of the Talents (Matthew 25:14–30) used the responsibilities of servants to explain accountability before God. The Parable of the Ten Virgins (Matthew 25:1–13) drew from common wedding customs to emphasize spiritual readiness for the return of Christ.

By connecting doctrine to life's events, Jesus made spiritual truth relatable and convicting. His listeners could no longer claim ignorance. The same scenes they witnessed daily now carried eternal meaning.

Teachers today must follow this example by using common experiences to clarify doctrinal truths. The principles of justification, sanctification, and obedience can be illustrated through relatable analogies—a courtroom verdict, a cleansing process, or a master-apprentice relationship.

However, the purpose is not merely to illustrate but to anchor doctrine in reality. Truth becomes transformative when it is seen in the context of daily living. By doing so, teachers imitate Jesus, who brought heaven's truth into the soil of earth's experience.

Avoiding Entertainment Without Meaning

While Jesus used captivating stories, He never used them for entertainment. His goal was always conviction, not amusement. Each parable carried eternal weight; each story demanded a response. There was no aimless storytelling in His ministry.

Modern teaching often errs by turning illustration into spectacle—seeking emotional engagement at the expense of spiritual edification. Jesus' stories, however, drew attention not to Himself as a storyteller but to His Father's truth. His parables provoked thought, stirred conscience, and called for decision.

After telling the Parable of the Sower, He declared, "He who has ears, let him hear" (Matthew 13:9). His words reminded listeners that stories were not ends in themselves but means to spiritual awakening. They concealed truth from the hardened while revealing it to the humble.

Teachers must therefore guard against illustrations that entertain but do not enlighten. Humor, emotion, or drama may engage attention, but if they fail to point to Christ, they fail their purpose. The teacher's task is not to captivate imagination alone but to convict the heart and conform the mind to Scripture.

Jesus' teaching balanced engagement with gravity. His stories drew listeners in but left them changed. The difference between entertainment and edification lies in whether the hearer walks away amused or awakened.

Discipleship Through Storytelling

Jesus used stories not only to convert unbelievers but also to train disciples. His parables and illustrations cultivated discernment, perseverance, and spiritual maturity. By requiring reflection, His stories strengthened faith and sharpened understanding.

In Matthew 13:10–17, when the disciples asked why He spoke in parables, Jesus explained that parables served a dual purpose: to reveal truth to the receptive and to conceal it from the hard-hearted. Those who sought understanding were granted more. Thus, storytelling became an instrument of discipleship—teaching the necessity of spiritual attentiveness.

Through repeated exposure to His stories, the disciples learned to interpret Scripture, apply wisdom, and see God's purposes in all things. Jesus did not merely tell them *what* to believe but taught them *how* to perceive truth. Each story trained their spiritual perception.

Modern discipleship must reclaim this principle. Stories remain powerful tools for shaping worldview and strengthening faith. Testimonies, case studies, and biblical narratives help believers internalize doctrine by seeing it in action. The teacher who uses stories to reinforce Scripture follows the same pattern as the Master, who turned truth into narrative and doctrine into dialogue.

In discipleship, stories do not replace exposition; they embody it. They give doctrine life and form, enabling learners to see faith in motion. Just as Jesus' parables trained His followers for ministry, stories anchored in Scripture can equip believers to apply truth in every sphere of life.

Jesus' use of illustrations and stories remains the highest example of divine communication. He turned ordinary language into revelation, transforming fields and families, banquets and boats into living sermons. His method dignified imagination, sanctified creativity, and proved that truth is most powerful when it is both seen and heard.

To imitate Jesus' use of illustration is to teach with vision—to make truth vivid, memorable, and meaningful. When we learn from His example, we move beyond explanation to revelation, helping others not merely to understand God's Word but to experience its living power.

Appendix A: Answering Hostility with Grace on Social Media

In an age when communication has moved from parchment and pulpit to pixels and posts, Christians must learn to represent Christ faithfully in digital spaces. Social media can magnify both opportunity and temptation—it enables the global spread of the gospel, yet it also amplifies hostility, pride, and division. As followers of the Great Teacher, our online words must reflect the same truth and grace that characterized Jesus' ministry.

Jesus never compromised truth to maintain peace, nor did He abandon kindness to defend truth. His speech was both direct and dignified, firm yet merciful. The believer who engages in online dialogue must imitate this balance. Every comment, reply, or post becomes a testimony of our faith. Whether correcting error, answering criticism, or defending doctrine, the goal is not to win arguments but to represent Christ.

This appendix provides biblical principles for navigating the hostility of online debate with wisdom, patience, and humility—transforming potential conflict into opportunity for witness.

Responding Without Compromising Truth

The first danger in hostile online environments is the temptation to soften or obscure truth to avoid confrontation. Yet Scripture commands believers to "speak the truth in love" (Ephesians 4:15), not to silence truth for the sake of popularity. Jesus never adjusted His message to appease His opponents. When confronted by the Pharisees, He remained unwavering in His proclamation of the Kingdom of God.

Online hostility often pressures believers to conform to cultural expectations of tolerance or relativism. But genuine love never compromises truth—it communicates it with compassion and conviction. To imitate Jesus is to respond with clarity, not confusion; with conviction, not concession.

However, firmness must never descend into harshness. The believer's response should always reflect both the authority of Scripture and the gentleness of Christ. Paul wrote, "Let your speech always be with grace, seasoned with salt, so that you will know how you should respond to each person" (Colossians 4:6).

Before posting or replying, one should prayerfully ask: *Will my words reveal the truth of God and reflect the character of Christ?* If either is absent, silence may speak louder than speech.

In every digital conversation, truth must remain central, but it must be wrapped in grace. Truth without love repels; love without truth misleads. The Christian communicator must hold both together, as Jesus did in every word He spoke.

Recognizing Traps in Online Debate

Jesus repeatedly faced verbal traps designed to discredit Him. The Pharisees and Sadducees often posed questions not out of sincerity but to ensnare Him in controversy. Yet He never allowed Himself to be manipulated into unwise or fruitless arguments. His discernment provides the perfect model for believers navigating online hostility.

When asked whether it was lawful to pay taxes to Caesar (Matthew 22:15–22), Jesus perceived their malice and answered with divine wisdom: "Render to Caesar the things that are Caesar's, and to God the things that are God's." His response transcended their trap by reframing the question according to eternal principle rather than political provocation.

Similarly, online debates often disguise themselves as intellectual inquiry while harboring ulterior motives. Many participants are not seeking truth but victory. Arguing with such individuals rarely yields fruit. Proverbs 26:4 warns, "Do not answer a fool according to his folly, or you will also be like him." Yet verse 5 adds, "Answer a fool as his folly deserves, that he not be wise in his own eyes." The balance lies in discerning *when* and *how* to respond.

Before engaging, ask: *Is this person genuinely seeking understanding, or simply seeking confrontation?* If the latter, restraint is often the wisest course. Jesus Himself remained silent before Herod (Luke 23:9) and spoke sparingly before Pilate (John 19:9–11). Silence, when guided by discernment, is not weakness but wisdom.

The believer must recognize that not every challenge deserves an answer, and not every accusation warrants defense. Our goal is to glorify God, not gratify pride.

Maintaining a Godly Tone Under Attack

Tone communicates as much as content. A true disciple's words must reflect Christ even when emotions are provoked. Jesus was insulted, mocked, and slandered, yet He never retaliated in anger. First Peter 2:23 records, "While being reviled, He did not revile in return; while suffering, He uttered no threats, but kept entrusting Himself to Him who judges righteously."

Social media, by its nature, fuels impulsive speech. Quick reactions often replace thoughtful responses. But spiritual maturity manifests in restraint. Proverbs 15:1 reminds us, "A gentle answer turns away wrath, but a harsh word stirs up anger."

To maintain a godly tone online, one must begin with a godly mindset. Prayer should precede posting. The believer must remember that every digital exchange occurs before the omnipresent eye of God. The question is not simply, *Am I right?* but *Am I righteous in how I respond?*

When attacked personally, Jesus modeled calm authority. When the soldiers mocked Him, He said nothing. When accused falsely, He let truth speak through His silence. When He did speak, His words were purposeful, redemptive, and restrained.

In following His example, believers must learn that tone either builds bridges or burns them. Harshness may win a point but lose a soul. Gentleness may lose an argument but win a heart. The goal is not verbal victory but spiritual influence.

Citing Scripture with Precision and Patience

Jesus' every response to opposition was anchored in Scripture. During His temptation in the wilderness (Matthew 4:1–11), He answered each of Satan's challenges with the words, "It is written." His authority rested not in personal opinion but in divine revelation.

Online discussions, especially those involving theology or morality, must likewise be grounded in the precise and faithful use of Scripture. Proof-texting or careless citation diminishes credibility and misrepresents truth. The Christian communicator must handle the Word of God "accurately" (2 Timothy 2:15), applying it with context, clarity, and humility.

Moreover, the presentation of Scripture must be patient. Many hostile interlocutors will distort or dismiss God's Word. Jesus did not react in frustration; He reasoned with clarity and allowed the truth to convict. Patience reflects confidence in the power of Scripture itself. Isaiah 55:11 promises that God's

Word "will not return to Me empty, without accomplishing what I desire."

In digital communication, precision requires restraint. Quoting Scripture is not a display of superiority but an act of service—offering divine truth to those who may not yet see it. Every verse must be shared in love, every reference explained carefully, and every correction delivered respectfully.

Teachers and apologists online must remember: authority lies not in eloquence but in faithfulness to the Word. Scripture, handled rightly, carries its own power to convict, comfort, and convert.

Turning Conflict into Gospel Opportunity

Jesus often turned confrontation into conversation and hostility into opportunity. When others sought to entrap Him, He used their questions to reveal God's truth. The Samaritan woman's defensiveness became an opening for the gospel (John 4). The Pharisees' accusations about healing on the Sabbath became lessons about mercy and divine authority (Luke 6:6–11).

Likewise, online hostility can become a doorway for witness. A critic's anger may mask spiritual hunger; a skeptic's mockery may conceal conviction.

The believer's calm and gracious reply can plant seeds of faith where hostility once reigned.

Paul exemplified this when he said, "My imprisonment in the cause of Christ has become well known throughout the whole praetorian guard... and most of the brethren, having confidence in the Lord because of my imprisonment, have far more courage to speak the word of God without fear" (Philippians 1:13–14). His hardship became evangelistic opportunity.

In the digital world, public hostility can serve the same purpose. A gracious, reasoned response to criticism not only addresses the attacker but also witnesses to all who observe the exchange. Many unbelievers read silently, forming opinions about Christ through the conduct of His followers.

The goal is not to silence critics but to glorify Christ. When truth is spoken in love and patience under provocation, it displays the transforming power of the gospel more clearly than any argument.

Protecting Your Testimony in Public Spaces

Every word spoken online contributes to one's testimony, for social media is a public stage. Jesus warned, "By your words you will be justified, and by your words you will be condemned" (Matthew 12:37). Digital communication is no exception. Believers must therefore exercise the same spiritual vigilance online that they would in person.

The apostle Peter exhorted Christians, "Keep your behavior excellent among the Gentiles, so that... they may because of your good deeds, as they observe them, glorify God" (1 Peter 2:12). Online interactions are visible deeds. They can either confirm or contradict our profession of faith.

Protecting one's testimony requires consistency. The same believer who proclaims Christ on Sunday must reflect His character on Monday's comment threads. Hypocrisy in digital form—boasting righteousness while displaying anger, sarcasm, or gossip—undermines the credibility of the gospel.

It also requires prudence. Not every controversy merits involvement. Proverbs 17:14 warns, "The beginning of strife is like letting out water, so abandon the quarrel before it breaks out." Sometimes wisdom lies in disengagement, trusting God to vindicate truth.

Ultimately, the believer's digital conduct must reflect the same call that governed Jesus' ministry: "Let your light shine before men in such a way that they may see your good works, and glorify your Father who is in heaven" (Matthew 5:16).

Social media may magnify hostility, but it can also magnify grace. Every interaction is an opportunity to display patience, humility, and faith. When believers respond with the mind of Christ and the wisdom of Scripture, even online hostility becomes a platform for His glory.

Bibliography

Andrews, E. (2018). *THE EARLY CHRISTIAN COPYISTS OF THE NEW TESTAMENT: The Making and Copying of the New Testament Books.* Cambridge: Christian Publishing House.

Andrews, E. (2020). *FROM SPOKEN WORDS TO SACRED TEXTS: Introduction-Intermediate New Testament Textual Studies.* Cambridge: Christian Publishing House.

Andrews, E. D. (2011). *AN INTRODUCTION TO BIBLE DIFFICULTIES So-Called Errors and Contradictions.* Cambridge: Christian Publishing House.

Andrews, E. D. (2012). *DIFFICULTIES IN THE BIBLE UPDATED: Updated and Expanded.* Cambridge, OH: Christian Publishing House.

Andrews, E. D. (2015). *CRISIS OF FAITH: Saving Those Who Doubt* . Cambridge, OH: Christian Publishing House.

Andrews, E. D. (2016). *HOMOSEXUALITY - THE BIBLE AND THE CHRISTIAN: Basic Bible Doctrines of the Christian Faith.* Cambridge, OH: Christian Publishing House.

Andrews, E. D. (2016). *INTERPRETING THE BIBLE: Introduction to Biblical Hermeneutics.* Cambridge, OH: Christian Publishing House.

Andrews, E. D. (2016). *THE BATTLE FOR THE CHRISTIAN MIND: Be Transformed by the Renewal of Your Mind.* Cambridge, OH: Christian Publishing House.

Andrews, E. D. (2016). *THE CHRISTIAN APOLOGIST: Always Being Prepared to Make a Defense [Second Edition].* Cambridge, OH: Christian Publishing House.

Andrews, E. D. (2016). *THE COMPLETE GUIDE to BIBLE TRANSLATION: Bible Translation Choices and Translation Principles [Second Edition]* . Cambridge: Christian Publishing House.

Andrews, E. D. (2016). *THE EVANGELISM HANDBOOK: How All Christians Can Effectively Share God's Word in Their Community, [SECOND EDITION].* Cambridge, OH: Christian Publishing House.

Andrews, E. D. (2017). *CONVERSATIONAL EVANGELISM: Defending the Faith, Reasoning from the Scriptures, Explaining and Proving, Instructing in Sound Doctrine, and Overturning False Reasoning [Second Edition].* Cambridge, OH: Christian Publishing House.

Andrews, E. D. (2017). *DEFENDING OLD TESTAMENT AUTHORSHIP: The Word of God Is Authentic and True.* Cambridge, OH: Christian Publishing House.

Andrews, E. D. (2017). *EARLY CHRISTIANITY IN THE FIRST CENTURY: Jesus' Witnesses to the Ends of the Earth.* Cambridge, OH: Christian Publishing House.

Andrews, E. D. (2017). *HOW TO STUDY YOUR BIBLE: Rightly Handling the Word of God.* Cambridge, OH: Christian Publishing House.

Andrews, E. D. (2017). *IS THE QURAN THE WORD OF GOD?: Is Islam the One True Faith.* Cambridge, OH: Christian Publishing House.

Andrews, E. D. (2018). *CHRISTIAN APOLOGETIC EVANGELISM: Reaching Hearts with the Art of Persuasion.* Cambridge, OH: Christian Publishing House.

Andrews, E. D. (2018). *REASONING FROM THE SCRIPTURES: Sharing CHRIST as You Help Others to Learn about the Mighty works of God.* Cambridge, Ohio: Christian Publishing House.

Andrews, E. D. (2018). *REASONING WITH THE WORLD'S VARIOUS RELIGIONS: Examining and Evangelizing Other Faiths.* Cambridge, OH: Christian Publishing House.

Andrews, E. D. (2018). *The CHURCH CURE: Overcoming Church Problems.* Cambridge, OH: Christian Publishing House.

Andrews, E. D. (2019). *MIRACLES: What Does the Bible Really Teach?* Cambridge, OH: Christian Publishing House.

Andrews, E. D. (2019). *THE READING CULTURE OF EARLY CHRISTIANITY: The Production, Publication, Circulation, and Use of Books in the Early Christian Church.* Cambridge, OH: Christian Publishing House.

Andrews, E. D. (2020). *INERRANCY OF SCRIPTURE: How Can We Believe Inerrancy of Scripture In the Originals When We Don't Have the Originals?* Cambridge, OH: Christian Publishing House.

Andrews, E. D. (2022). *THE QUEST FOR THE HISTORICAL JESUS: Are Doubts About*

Jesus Justified? Cambridge, OH: Christian Publishing House.

Andrews, E. D. (2023). *ARCHAEOLOGY & THE NEW TESTAMENT.* Cambridge, Ohio: Christian publishing House.

Andrews, E. D. (2023). *ARCHAEOLOGY & THE OLD TESTAMENT.* Cambridge, Ohio: Christian Publishing House.

Andrews, E. D. (2023). *BIBLICAL EXEGESIS: Biblical Criticism on Trial.* Cambridge, OH: Christian Publishing House.

Andrews, E. D. (2023). *CHRISTIAN APOLOGETICS: Answering the Tough Questions: Evidence and Reason in Defense of the Faith.* Cambridge, Ohio: Christian Publishing House.

Andrews, E. D. (2023). *HOW WE GOT THE BIBLE.* Cambridge, OH: Christian Publishing House.

Andrews, E. D. (2023). *ISLAM & THE QURAN: Examining the Quran & Islamic Teachings.* Cambridge, OH: Christian Publishing House.

Andrews, E. D. (2023). *ISLAMIC ESCHATOLOGY: Awaiting Al-Mahdi—The Twelfth Imam and the Future of Islam.* Cambridge, OH: Christian Publishing House.

Andrews, E. D. (2023). *JOHN CALVIN: A Solitary Quest for the Truth.* Cambridge, Ohio: Christian Publishing House.

Andrews, E. D. (2023). *THE BIBLE ON TRIAL: Examining the Evidence for Being Inspired, Inerrant, Authentic, and True.* Cambridge, Ohio: Christian Publishing House.

Andrews, E. D. (2023). *THE MACCABEES: The Hasmonaean Dynasty between Malachi and Matthew.* Cambridge, OH: Christian Publishing House.

Andrews, E. D. (2024). *BATTLE PLANS: A Game Plan for Answering Objections to the Christian Faith.* Cambridge, OH: Christian Publishing House.

Andrews, E. D. (2024). *CHRISTIAN APOLOGISTS OF THE SECOND CENTURY: Christian Defenders of the Faith.* Cambridge, OH: Christian Publishing House.

Andrews, E. D. (2024). *CHRISTIAN THEOLOGY: The Christian's Ultimate Guide to Learning from the Bible.* Cambridge, OH: Christian Publishing House.

Andrews, E. D. (2024). *CREATION AND COSMOS: A Journey Through Creation, Science, and the*

Origins of Life. Cambridge, OH: Christian Publishing House.

Andrews, E. D. (2024). *DO WE STILL NEED A LITERAL BIBLE?: Discover the Truth about Literal Bibles.* Cambridge, OH: Christian Publishing House.

Andrews, E. D. (2024). *FAITH UNDER FIRE: Refuting the Top 30 Arguments Atheists Make Against Christianity.* Cambridge, OH: Christian Publishing House.

Andrews, E. D. (2024). *HELL: All You Need to Know About Hell.* Cambridge, OH: Christian Publishing House.

Andrews, E. D. (2024). *REASON MEETS FAITH: Addressing and Refuting Atheism's Challenges to Christianity.* Cambridge, OH: Christian Publishing House.

Andrews, E. D. (2024). *THE BABYLONIAN EMPIRE.* Cambridge, OH: Christian Publishing House.

Andrews, E. D. (2024). *THE BATTLE OF JERICHO—Myth or Fact?* Cambridge, OH: Christian Publishing House.

Andrews, E. D. (2024). *THE ENCYCLOPEDIA OF CHRISTIAN APOLOGETICS: The Resource for Pastors, Teachers, and Believers.* Cambridge: Christian Publishing House.

Andrews, E. D. (2024). *THE HISTORICAL ADAM & EVE: Reconciling Faith and Fact in Genesis.* Cambridge, OH: Christian Publishing House.

Andrews, E. D. (2024). *THE HISTORICAL JESUS: The Death, Burial, and Resurrection of Jesus Christ.* Cambridge, OH: Christian Publishing House.

Andrews, E. D. (2024). *UNDERSTANDING THE HITTITES: Biblical History, Archaeological Discoveries, and Etymological Clarifications.* Cambridge, OH: Christian Publishing House.

Andrews, E. D. (2025). *A FRESH LOOK AT PAUL'S THEOLOGY: Biblical Theology as Revealed through Paul.* Cambridge, OH: Christian Publishing House.

Andrews, E. D. (2025). *ATHEISM: What Will You Say to an Atheist.* Cambridge, OH: Christian Publishing House.

Andrews, E. D. (2025). *BIBLE DIFFICULTIES: How to Approach Difficulties In the Bible.* Cambridge, OH: Christian Publishing House.

Andrews, E. D. (2025). *BIBLICAL WORDS AND THEIR MEANING: An Introduction to Lexical Semantics.* Cambridge, OH: Christian Publishing House.

Andrews, E. D. (2025). *CAN WE TRUST THE BIBLE?* Cambridge, OH: Christian Publishing House.

Andrews, E. D. (2025). *DISCOVERING GENESIS ANSWERS: Exploring the Historical and Cultural Contexts of Genesis, One Insight at a Time (Answers from Genesis).* Cambridge, OH: Christian Publishing House.

Andrews, E. D. (2025). *DISCOVERING GENESIS ANSWERS: Tackling Tough Questions in Genesis: One Solution at a Time (Answers from Genesis).* Cambridge, OH: Christian Publishing House.

Andrews, E. D. (2025). *DISCOVERING GENESIS ANSWERS: Unveiling the Truths of Creation, One Answer at a Time (Answers from Genesis).* Cambridge, OH: Christian Publishing House.

Andrews, E. D. (2025). *EARLY CHRISTIANITY: Exploring Backgrounds, Historical Settings, and Cultures.* Cambridge, OH: Christian Publishing House.

Andrews, E. D. (2025). *IMMORTALITY OF THE SOUL: The Birth of the Doctrine.* Cambridge, OH: Christian Publishing House.

Andrews, E. D. (2025). *ISLAMIC IDEOLOGICAL JIHAD: Islamic-Funded, Islamic-Indoctrinated, Western Youth.* Cambridge, OH: Christian Publishing House.

Andrews, E. D. (2025). *JOSEPHUS & THE NEW TESTAMENT: Evidence from the First-Century Jewish Historian on Key Biblical Figures, Groups, and Events.* Cambridge, OH: Christian Publishing House.

Andrews, E. D. (2025). *LINGUISTICS AND THE BIBLICAL TEXT: Unlocking Scripture Through the Science of Language.* Cambridge, OH: Christian Publishing House.

Andrews, E. D. (2025). *OVERCOMING BIBLE DIFFICULTIES: Answers to the So-Called Errors and Contradictions [Second Edition].* Cambridge: Christian Publishing House.

Andrews, E. D. (2025). *PROVING GOD'S EXISTENCE.* Cambridge, OH: Christian Publishing House.

Andrews, E. D. (2025). *THE ANDREWS BIBLE BLUEPRINT: Unlocking Scripture's Truth,*

History, and Wisdom. Cambridge, OH: Christian Publishing House.

Andrews, E. D. (2025). *THE ENCYCLOPEDIA OF THE TEXT OF THE NEW TESTAMENT: The Resource for Pastors, Teachers, and Believers.* Cambridge, OH: Christian Publishing House.

Andrews, E. D. (2025). *THE FACES OF ISLAM: Faith or Facade: Decoding Islam's Strategies.* Cambridge, OH: Christian Publishing House.

Andrews, E. D. (2025). *THE GUIDE TO SPIRITUAL WARFARE: Standing Firm in the Armor of God Against the Schemes of the Devil.* Cambridge, OH: Christian Publishing House.

Andrews, E. D. (2025). *THE STONES SPEAK: Biblical Archaeology and the Reliability of the Bible.* Cambridge, OH: Christian Publishing House.

Andrews, E. D. (2025). *WONDERFULLY MADE: Wonderful Are God's Works.* Cambridge, OH: Christian Publishing House.

Andrews, E. D. (2025). *YOUR YOUTH: The Young Christian's Guide to Making Right Choices.* Cambridge, OH: Christian Publishing House.

Beattie, F. (2022). *CHRISTIAN APOLOGETICS [Annotated]: The Rational Vindication of Christianity.* Cambridge, OH: Christian Publishing House.

Kephart, E. B. (2022). *APOLOGETICS Annotated: A Treatise on Christian Evidences - [Annotated].* Cambridge, OH: Christian Publishing House.

www.ingramcontent.com/pod-product-compliance
Lightning Source LLC
Chambersburg PA
CBHW072344090426
42741CB00012B/2917

* 9 7 8 1 9 4 9 5 8 6 8 3 1 *